FROM THE LIBRARY OF
FLOE HOWARD

WHERE
THE GRIZZLY
WALKS

WHERE
THE GRIZZLY
WALKS

Bill Schneider

MOUNTAIN PRESS PUBLISHING COMPANY
MISSOULA, MONTANA

Library of Congress Cataloging in Publication Data

Schneider, Bill.
  Where the grizzly walks.

  1. Grizzly bear. I. Title.
QL737.C27S28   599'.7358   76-58451
ISBN O-87842-067-3

For Rusty and Greg, my two sons.

May they grow up and see a wild grizzly.

ACKNOWLEDGEMENTS

It's with some reservations that I list only my name as author of *Where the Grizzly Walks,* because so many people helped this book become reality.

Most helpful and, of course, essential were the dedicated wildlife professionals who guided me in getting the complex facts down accurately. I wish to especially thank John Cada, John Craighead, Ken Greer, Charles Jonkel, Clifford Martinka, Larry Roop, and Frank Singer. Others from the wildlife profession who helped were Steve Bayless, Doug Chadwick, Glen Cole, Frank DeShon, Joe Egan, Albert Erickson, Sarah Johnson, Stephen Herrero, Maurice Hornocker, Richard Knight, A. Starker Leopold, Larry Mullen, Jim Posewitz, and Ken Walcheck.

Rick Applegate, Bill Cunningham, Clif Merritt, Richard Moy, Leonard Lee Rue III, and K. Ross Toole offered invaluable advice after reviewing draft copies of the book.

In the seemingly endless process of outlining, researching, typing, editing, and proofreading the manuscript, I'm indebted to Caroline Cunningham, Kay Ellerhoff, Louis Flaccus, Sara Gartland, Tom Kotynski, Russ McKee, Harriet Meloy and the Montana Historical Society, Dave Sumner, and the Wilderness Institute at the University of Montana. Gathering the massive pile of essential research information would have been impossible without Kathy Brown and the other friendly, hard working employees of the Montana State Library.

The splendid photography came from Bob Anderson, Lynne Bama, Jon Cates, Gene Colling, Beth Givens, Interagency Study Team, Jerry Manley (jacket photo), Tom McBride, Montana Department of Fish and Game, Doug O'looney, Dave Shors, Rick Trembath, Ted Trueblood, U.S. Forest Service, and Utah Division of Wildlife.

There were so many sincere people, all concerned about the grizzly, that it's pleasant to write this and bring back memories. I apologize if I forgot somebody.

Finally, the book wouldn't have been finished without Marnie, my wife, who has more patience than I believed possible. And where would I have been without Rusty and Greg, my beloved boys? Their very presence kept me going.

Bill Schneider

CONTENTS

Doug O'looney photo.

THE GRIZZLY
IS MORE THAN A BEAR

The day I saw my first grizzly something told me I was seeing more than a bear.

While crossing a wild mountain stream, the large grizzly was silhouetted against one of the most outstanding scenes the American wilderness has ever offered, an ideal setting of seclusion and serenity. Here was the summit of the wild kingdom, a majestic animal endowed with dignity, courage, strength, and ingenuity, against a backdrop of extraordinary beauty.

For a few seconds I watched the grizzly, truly the king of the American wilderness, go about the business of life. Then the bear somehow sensed my presence and quickly melted into the nearby forest. The image remained permanently etched in my mind — a picture of nature at its best, the way it should work, but seldom does, in modern America.

But I had been witnessing more than America's most magnificent wild animal amid beautiful scenery. Landscape and bear joined as a fading symbol of the western wilderness that pioneers fought so hard to conquer — and which, regrettably, modern America is still fighting to conquer, even though it exists only in scattered traces. I had viewed a remnant of the nation's past glory.

Lewis and Clark challenged the western wilderness in 1804-6. Among their notable discoveries was the great "white bear" inhabiting the rugged breaks and ocean-like plains of the Missouri River drainage. The adventurers painted a vivid picture of an awesome and vicious beast — a threat to man. Later, their journals were glamorized and often repeated.

Soon, mountain men began wandering throughout grizzly country, naming the big bear "Old Ephraim." They fought him, killed him, but admired him, some of them, like Lewis and Clark, putting their experiences with the grizzly down on paper to excite future generations. As a result, Americans almost automatically associate the grizzly with ferocity and danger. Today, children unconsciously grow up fearing the grizzly.

Writers and film makers too frequently, and often inaccurately, portray the grizzly as the last word of evil. Something about large predators stirs man's deepest fears. Bloody meetings between man and bear have remarkable news value, and because the press repeatedly over-reacts to these confrontations, news of a mauling spreads with flashing speed. And people are slow to forget.

In 1967, two young women were killed by grizzlies in Montana's Glacier National Park. In 1972, a young male camper was fatally mauled in Yellowstone National Park. In 1976, another young woman was dragged from her tent and killed in Montana's Glacier Park. In the same year, two hikers died —one in Canada's Glacier National Park and another in Alaska's Glacier Bay National Monument—after being mauled by grizzlies.

Could these tragedies have been prevented? Are the national parks too dangerous? Are the parks for people or for bears? Can man and grizzly co-exist in the parks? Or should these natural areas be cleared of grizzlies to make them "safe for people," as some authorities have advocated?

This tragic part of the story has been overplayed — to the bear's detriment. True, the grizzly is powerful and unpredictable, a threat to the careless and unprepared. But America has never been introduced to the real grizzly — a curious and cautious creature that rarely attacks man or destroys his property.

Also stealing more than its share of press coverage is the great debate between Yellowstone Park officials and Drs. Frank and John Craighead, two distinguished wildlife scientists. The Craighead brothers have claimed park policies are wiping out the grizzly. By 1990, the Yellowstone grizzly will be reduced to bitter history, the Craigheads insist.

The National Park Service has countered the Craighead evaluation, stating that park management reflects careful consideration of the bear's problems. Bear numbers will soon stabilize if opportunities for the grizzly to scavenge for human garbage are cut off, park officials claim.

Finally, the bear is enmeshed in a national controversy over hunting. Although the U.S. Department of the Interior has officially classified the grizzly (south of Canada) as a "threatened species" under the U.S. Endangered Species Act of 1973, hunting continues on a limited basis. And grizzly hunting, which seems inconsistent with efforts to save the great bear, infuriates individuals and organizations devoted to the preservation of wildlife.

These three controversies — grizzly maulings, the Yellowstone debate, and hunting — have dominated media coverage. Unfortunately, this emphasis has shielded more serious problems from public view. Even though the grizzly has received its share of limelight, most Americans still haven't been told what really threatens the bear or what they can do about it.

Civilization's lemming-like drive into the grizzly's last refuges endangers the silvertip more than any other factor, and perhaps all other factors. With bulldozers, gondolas, recreational subdivisions, logging roads, power lines, and mines, man steadily advances. And the big bear steadily retreats. Here is a species in unquestionable jeopardy, especially when some people — particularly westerners — prefer to see the bear plunge over the brink of extinction to make the forests safe and to protect the livestock.

To document the grizzly's dilemma, I deal with specific issues and developments. They may seem like regional problems, each having little impact on the overall grizzly population. But a thousand battles make a war, and wars can't be won without winning battles.

Wildlife preservationists have mounted a national "save the grizzly" movement. Most of these people will never see a wild grizzly, nor do they expect to. If they all did, they would crowd the bear out. Yet, many of these people, who desperately want to help the big bear, understand that if the silvertip's salvation is left to westerners, the end is near.

The recent debate over classifying the grizzly as a "threatened species" brought almost 6,000 letters into Interior Department offices. Most of these letters urged full protection for the bear, the only serious argument against protection coming from the Rocky Mountain West, where the last grizzlies in the Continental United States range. This was further emphasized when the Interior Department began delineating "critical" grizzly habitat, as required by the Endangered Species Act. Western opposition was violent and omnipresent.

Yes, conservationists nationwide know that the bear desperately needs help. But they also understand what the grizzly represents, recognizing his symbolic value as a source of national pride.

Thus, this becomes more than a book about a bear. It becomes a book about people and their life-styles. What happens to the wilderness king will be felt outside his realm. The impact will be subtle, but nonetheless noticeable, for the grizzly's plight is actually part of a larger problem affecting everyone. Saving the grizzly won't totally solve society's dilemmas of industrial growth, wasteful living, congestion, pollution, and an expanding population, but it's an appropriate place to start. (The goal — stabilizing or increasing the grizzly population — is certainly much easier to reach than solutions to the complex problems of a technological society.) Basically, the silvertip's salvation rests on protecting remaining habitat and in changing long-established attitudes toward the big bear.

Although many people view the grizzly as insignificant in their everyday lives, this bear is undeniably linked to aspects of living that are "close to home," so to speak. Where the grizzly walks, the land remains relatively untouched by man. One can look up and clearly see North America's backbone, the Continental Divide, where towering crags send flashing waters seaward. Here, a small part of a large nation has escaped technology and maintained its natural integrity.

Where the grizzly walks, one finds free rivers, gem-like lakes, cloud-brushing peaks, mysterious stillness, and the perfection of camas petals; kaleidoscopic wildflower blankets, trackless snowfalls, the coyote's midnight serenade, cutthroat trout, and the uncommon beauty of a crest of purest blue. Vast wildernesses, wild creatures, stately pines, and untainted breezes blend in harmony under sky free of pollution plumes.

Over this high country, the grizzly bear majestically marches, and the song of the wilderness resounds with freedom as sweet as life and as old and proud as the mountain summits.

Now, however, the grizzly's freedom is being checked, and the spirit of the wilderness is slipping away, its song perhaps fading to a requiem. And with the loss of this wilderness heritage will go a large part of an elusive condition everyone is seeking, a high quality of life.

Wildlife acts as an indicator of a quality environment for man. As he upsets the delicate structure of nature and as wildlife habitat disappears, human habitat becomes less desirable and indeed, steadily less livable. To most people, this means more congestion, more pollution, more crime, more social strife, more noise, less open space, and less recreational opportunity. Thus, this can't be only a book about bears. It must also deal with people — their life styles, their government, their land, and their dreams.

Never again will the grizzly's song of freedom be heard loud and clear — as in decades past. Too much wilderness has gone to accommodate the bear's only enemy, man. But there is still a chance to save the great bear in the last shreds of his once vast range south of Canada's border. There is even a better chance in the undeveloped expanses of Canada and Alaska. However, we won't preserve the wild grizzly anywhere without changing land use policy and public attitudes.

Future generations will deeply appreciate the grizzly's presence and likely understand what this really means to their society. But this generation will make the decisions which make the grizzly's future possible. Hopefully, our heirs will know where the grizzly walks.

Doug O'looney photo.

Chapter 1

MEET
THE GRIZZLY

Taxonomists put the grizzly in the Order Carnivora. However, this label, "carnivore," can be misleading. To most people, it means "meat-eater" or "predator," both of which miss the mark. The grizzly eats mostly plant matter — berries, roots, succulent forbs, etc. In fact, one is more likely to see the big bear grazing like an elk than stalking like a lion.

Perhaps "giant meat-and-vegetable-eater" most appropriately describes the grizzly, or to be more technical, the grizzly is an omnivore that feeds on both plant and animal matter — whatever comes easiest. This omnivorous diet occasionally brings the grizzly into garbage dumps to feed on human refuse. This invariably results in a bitter bear/man conflict, in which the grizzly almost always loses.

The grizzly eats meat, but mostly carrion or small animals such as ground squirrels. He often prefers to bury a dead animal until it becomes putrid

1

before he dines. Normally, he remains in the vicinity of the buried carrion, returning often to feed, until it has been completely consumed.

The grizzly rarely preys on large animals such as elk, deer, moose, or domestic livestock. He occasionally kills large animals, usually in the spring, when young or weak animals are more easily captured. But this type of prey accounts for only a small fraction of his year-round diet. Likewise, fish are important in the grizzly's diet but only in specific geographical areas such as the Alaska salmon streams. In Yellowstone Park, grizzlies have traditionally feasted on winter-killed (or weakened) elk. The park routinely produces more elk than the available range can support, resulting in periodic die-offs.

Omnivore, carnivore, or whatever word is used, the grizzly is unquestionably impressive. His long fur and bulky body make him appear even larger than he actually is, leading to frequent exaggerations of over 1,000 and even up to 2,000 pounds.

In truth, full-grown male grizzlies average 350-800 pounds, with a rare old-timer reaching 1,000 pounds. Females and young adults are somewhat smaller.

His size ranks the grizzly *(Ursus arctos horribilis)* as the largest member of the Order Carnivora, south of Canada. Farther north, both the Alaskan brown or Kodiak bear *(Ursus arctos middendorffi)* and polar bear *(Ursus maritimus)* can outweigh the grizzly.[1]

Old Ephraim's large size is reflected in the amount of country he needs to survive. Home range estimates go as high as 168 square miles, although the ranges are usually smaller, about 10-40 square miles. Over this territory, the bear travels widely. Although biologists know of the grizzly's nomadic behavior, the reasons for some of it remain a mystery.

The silvertip moves slowly with his massiveness, yet smoothly and gracefully, like a true monarch. He has a tireless lope, which allows him to travel tremendous distances with ease. And when it's needed, he has a blinding burst of speed. In fact, the grizzly's speed is often underestimated, as the bear looks too husky to be a sprinter. However, for a short distance, the grizzly can outrun a race horse.

Even with his impressive physical attributes, the grizzly isn't unmistakable in the wild world. Differentiating between the grizzly and his smaller cousin,

---

[1]Zoologists first described the grizzly of the western continental U.S. in the early 1800s. They gave the bear the scientific name *Ursus horribilis*. Later, the North American subspecies of the circumpolar species, *Ursus arctos,* was separated into *Ursus arctos horribilis* (the grizzly), *Ursus arctos middendorffi* (the Alaska brown or Kodiak bear), and *Ursus arctos richardsoni* (the barren ground grizzly). In Eurasia, *Ursus arctos* is further split into several more subspecies.

the black bear *(Ursus americanus),* can be confusing.

Mountain guides sometimes tell their clients, "If you see a black bear, you may wonder if it's a black or a grizzly. But if you see a grizzly, there will be no doubt in your mind." With full-grown grizzlies at close range, this advice may hold true. However, young adult grizzlies can closely resemble black bears which have a brown or cinnamon color phase. Grizzlies vary from almost white to yellow to dark brown to black.

The grizzly has a prominent hump on his back formed by the powerful musculature of his forelegs. He also has long claws (4 inches or longer) that usually show up in the track and a large head with a slightly dished face. The black bear has no hump, shorter claws that don't show up in the track, and a smaller head. The grizzly's track is also much larger (10 inches or longer) than the black bear's.

In search of a sure-fire difference, seasoned woodsmen have been known to quip, "You know it's a grizzly if it can't climb up the tree after you. If it does, don't worry. It's a black bear."

This joke comes from the adult grizzly's inability to climb trees. The grizzly grubs for food with his long claws, making them dull and unusable for tree climbing. On the other hand, the black bear's shorter, sharper claws allow tree climbing throughout his life. Grizzly cubs can climb trees, but they quickly lose this ability.

Some grizzlies have white-tipped hair on their upper bodies, giving them a "grizzled" appearance, from which came the names "grizzly," "silvertip," and "white bear." However, the absence of this beautiful pelage doesn't mean an animal is a black bear, since many grizzlies lack this characteristic coloring.

"One day a leaf fell in the woods," one early observer noted. "The eagle saw it. The deer heard it. And the bear smelled it." This story, in a mythic way, emphasizes the advanced sense of smell of the grizzly which relies heavily on his nose to detect danger and find food. Although his sense of hearing is also excellent, his vision — at least in older bears — is weak.

Grizzlies usually mature sexually in their fourth year at the earliest and sometimes later. Mating occurs in June and July, which is almost the only time grizzlies can be seen together except for a female with young. In natural situations, the grizzly ranks among the most solitary and anti-social of animals. After mating, Old Ephraim settles down to fatten up for the long mountain winter.

Grizzlies usually enter their dens in November or December. Females normally bed down for the winter before males. However, bears aren't true hibernators. True hibernation requires a significant drop in body temperature and respiration rate, neither of which occurs in bears. True hibernators such as ground squirrels fall into a deep sleep and can hardly be roused — even purposely. Conversely, grizzlies can remain active all winter. At times, they even leave the den for a stroll and then return for the rest of the winter.

Cubs are born in January or February. Considering their massive parents, the cubs are amazingly small — only about 14 ounces at birth. They leave the den that spring at about 10-20 pounds and grow to around 100 pounds before entering the den again the next winter.

Young ones stay with their mother until June of their second year. Then they are abandoned. Often, the cast-off cubs may "hang around" for a few months, following their mother or staying in the immediate vicinity, reluctant to break the bonds completely. Biologists call this arrangement a "loose family group."

Because they keep their cubs for two years, grizzlies can only reproduce every other year — although reproduction is often more infrequent. Litters usually consist of two cubs, but can vary from one to four.

Like his diet and color, Old Ephraim's habitat is diverse, varying with vegetative cover, elevation, climate, slope, and other physical factors. There is one common factor, though. To be grizzly habitat, the land must be relatively untouched and unused by man. The big bear occasionally ventures into developed areas, but only on the fringe of a core of wilderness. Without these vast tracts of untrammeled land, Old Ephraim can't survive.

Land can be wild and still be without the grizzly. Indeed, many millions of acres of western wild land are without grizzlies. Some of these remote regions historically supported viable populations, and nobody knows why the great bear was exterminated in one area, but survived in the next. The pressure to rid the West of this "horrible" bear was similar everywhere in the frontier days.

For instance, Montana's Bob Marshall Wilderness retained a sizeable grizzly population, but the Selway/Bitterroot Wilderness, only 125 air miles away on the Idaho/Montana border, has apparently lost its king. Both wilderness areas, alike in many respects, are large enough (more than a million acres) to support grizzlies. And historical records indicate the Selway/Bitterroot had a large grizzly population. So why didn't Old Ephraim persist there?

Wildlife professionals believe the quality of the habitat has much to do with whether bears have survived in a particular area. Some vital habitat ingredients (or combination of ingredients) may have disappeared in the

4

Such characteristics as a large head with slightly dished face, prominent hump on the back, long claws, and the sheer bulk of the massive frame help differentiate the grizzly from his smaller cousin, the black bear. Jon Cates photo.

The black bear can be distinguished from the grizzly by the absence of the prominent hump on the back, shorter claws that rarely show up in the track, and most often, a smaller head in comparison to the rest of the body. Dave Shors photo.

Selway/Bitterroot but endured in the Bob Marshall. But they can only guess about the specifics.

A figure of power, majesty, and freedom, the grizzly rules supreme among the native fauna, fearing only man and larger bears. He is noble, defiant, vigorous, mysterious, enduring, courageous, long-lived, mobile, brawny, intelligent, cautious, agile, curious, solitary, fun-loving, and individualistic — traits often admired by man. With his superior physical and mental qualities, the grizzly undoubtedly deserves the title, king of the American wilderness.

Chapter 2

A BEAR
IS WISER
THAN A MAN

The story of man's encounter with the grizzly bear is played and replayed in vivid melodrama throughout history. Consequently, the awesome white bear has become enmeshed in American folklore.

Although heavy on fiction, historical references are, to say the least, colorful, and millions still eagerly read the history of the great bear. This is fortunate, for without understanding the past, one can hardly comprehend the future. If we ignore history, we are destined to repeat it.

"Permanent grizzly ranges and permanent wilderness areas are, of course, two names for one problem," agrees Aldo Leopold in his conservation classic, *A Sand County Almanac*. "Enthusiasm about either requires a long view of conservation, and a historical perspective. Only those able to see the pageant of evolution can be expected to value its theater, the wilderness, or its outstanding achievement, the grizzly."

7

Perhaps more than any other animal, bears inspired native Americans — and especially the western tribes. The high place given the grizzly in Indian life and religion is understandable, however. Certainly, brutal battles between the big bear and Indians, armed only with primitive weapons, bred respect for the grizzly. Many tribes went even further — actually worshipping the grizzly and moving the bear to a level of semi-divinity.

Indians and grizzlies hunted the same habitat, fed on many of the same foods, and to many early observers even resembled each other. When erect, the bear walked like a man, but he was mightier and, some natives felt, wiser. "The bear is wiser than a man," an old Abinaki Indian once theorized, "because man does not know how to live all winter without eating anything."

This sometimes bloody, sometimes benevolent relationship between grizzly and Indian is fascinating. America's natives linked land and people as one and personified wild creatures, often referring to the grizzly as "grandfather," "cousin," "brother," or "ancestor." Since Indian culture isn't the subject of this book, however, a small sampling of this exciting literature will suffice.

The Great Spirit made Mount Shasta first of all.[1] That was thousands of summers ago, when there was no life of any kind upon the earth. There were no animals, for there was nothing for them to eat; and no birds, for there were no trees or flowers in which they might build their nests; and no fish, for the streams and rivers had not yet been made. But one day, as the Great Spirit looked down from his home up among the stars, he decided to come down to have a closer look at the earth. So he pushed down snow and ice through a hole in the blue sky, until he had made a mountain so great that it was easy to step down upon it from a big white cloud.

As he stood on top of the great mountain and looked around, the Great Spirit saw that the earth was entirely barren and lifeless. He decided to make the earth beautiful and create living things to enjoy it. Walking down out of the snow, he put his fingers onto the bare ground, and green trees, grass, and flowers instantly sprang up and began spreading into forests that quickly covered the valleys and low hills. Then he told the sun to shine a little more brightly, to melt some of the snow on the great mountains, just enough so that the water would run down to nurture the forests and the flowers. With the end of his walking

[1]Reprinted from *The Beast That Walks Like a Man*, by Harold McCracken, with permission from the University of Oklahoma Press, Norman. 1955.

8

stick he marked out a place for the streams and rivers, which began carrying water out to fill the sea. Then he broke off the small end of his walking stick, which he crushed into small bits in his hand, and, casting these into the streams, they became fish which swam away to spawn. Picking some leaves from the trees, he held them in the palm of his hand and, blowing them into the air, they became birds of many kinds which flew away singing, to build their nests. After this, very pleased with what he had done, the Great Spirit broke off some more of his walking stick and, casting larger bits of it about, they became animals of many kinds. He made them of many sizes, some weak and some swift of foot, and each one a little stronger or a little swifter than others, so they would each have a good chance of survival. And when he came to the large end of his walking stick, the heavy part that he always held in his right hand, he held it thoughtfully for some time, deciding just what sort of creature he should make out of this last sturdy piece; and then he made an animal that was to be mightier than any of the others and was to rule over all the rest. This was the grizzly bear. But, when this animal took form and life, it was so strong and aggressive that the Great Spirit had to climb hurriedly back to the mountaintop, to find a safe place to rest after performing all his labors of creating life upon the earth.

(Thus begins the story of creation as related by the Shasta and Modoc Indians, who lived in the region which is today northern California and southern Oregon. These people had been old residents there for hundreds and hundreds of years before Sir Francis Drake's crew of the *Golden Hind,* on June 17, 1579, "landed in what is now Marin County, California. . . just north of the Golden Gate and lying between San Francisco Bay and the broad Pacific," and they claimed the territory for Queen Elizabeth of England. The Spanish came later, built their missions, and took possession; and then they lost California to the aggressive frontier determination of the United States. But the Shastas and Modocs knew little or nothing about what was going on beyond the shadow of towering Mount Shasta and the limited horizon of the wooded mountain ridges around them. They had their first contact with the white men in the early part of the nineteenth century, when an occasional trapper came into their territory; but the development of gold mining in the 1850s and '60s, and the shortly following conquest of the upper Sacramento Valley by white settlers in a greedy scramble for new farm lands, overran the ancestral domain of these red men and brought about the hasty processes of their extinction as a race. The grizzly bears in that district have also become a memory of the past. But the great Mount Shasta still rises in all its magnitude and beauty, and the primeval story which it inspired so many centuries before the coming of

9

the destructive white man still survives as one of the classics of Indian legendry.)

The Great Spirit, when he first came down from the sky, made the earth such a beautiful place that he decided to stay for a while. So he converted Mount Shasta into a great tepee, built a fire inside to make it a pleasant place to live, and brought down his family from up among the stars. The fire glowed upward out of the tepee top against the dark sky at night, and by day the smoke rose lazily to drift with the clouds. The Indians knew this was so, because their ancestors had seen it when the fire and the smoke were there many hundreds of summers ago.

It was not very long after the Great Spirit brought his family down to live in Mount Shasta that one day his youngest and fairest daughter wandered down into the woodlands that spread far out around the base of the mountain. It was in the springtime, when all the flowers were in blossom; the birds were all singing and building their nests; the salmon were coming up the streams from the sea to spawn, and animals were with their newborn young.

The beautiful little girl wandered farther and farther, with the spring breezes blowing through her long red hair and putting an extra bit of color into the soft skin of her cheeks. She had been so fascinated by the fragrance of the flowers and the forest, and the songs of the birds, that when the end of the day approached she could not remember the way back to her home. But she was not afraid, and finally, becoming very tired, she crawled under the spreading branches of a big tree and lay down to rest.

Not far from where the fairest child of the Great Spirit lay down a family of grizzly bears had their home. The mother bear had lately brought forth, and the father was out procuring food for the newly born. It should be remembered that in this time of so long ago the grizzly bears were somewhat different than we know them today. They were covered with the same heavy coat of hair, had their long sharp claws, and lived in caves; but they walked erect on two feet, talked among themselves in a language of their own, just as humans do today, and they used heavy clubs for weapons instead of their claws and teeth. Beasts that they were, and arrogant rulers of all the animal world, they had quite a pleasant family life.

As the father grizzly returned home, with his club on his shoulder and a young elk carried under his left arm, he saw the beautiful little girl lying under the tree, with her long red hair partly covering her bare shoulders. Not knowing what to make of this soft, gentle creature, he took her home to his wife, who was very wise in all such matters. The old grizzly mother was not only wise and kind, but she ran their household pretty

10

much as she chose to. "We will keep this strange child," she said in a very determined voice. "I will share my breast with her and we will bring her up with the other children, and maybe some good will come of it. But we must never mention anything about it to anyone else."

And so it was. The little daughter of the Great Spirit was raised in this family of grizzly bears. The mother bear cared for her, just as she did for her own children; and the father went out through the forest with his club on his shoulder, to provide food for all of them.

Then came the time when all the young were grown up and must start families of their own. "Our son must have a wife," the old mother grizzly said one evening as they were all gathered together. "It should be our adopted daughter, the fair one with the pink skin and the long red hair, whom your father found under the tree." This met with the approval of everyone. "You are a very wise wife," said the father bear. "You are a very kind mother," said the girl. So the father went out with his club over his shoulder to get some special meat for the marriage feast.

All the other grizzlies were now told about it, and they came from many miles around to make the happy event a most memorable one. They celebrated as one family, for they were all very pleased, and together they built a great tepee for the pretty red princess and her grizzly bear husband. They built it close to that of her father's, and it can still be seen and is now called Little Mount Shasta.

The marriage was a happy one, and many children were born. The children, being partly the flesh and blood of the Great Spirit and partly that of the grizzly bear, were somewhat different from either of their parents. Their skin was reddish and bare, like that of their mother, and the hair of their heads was long but black, like that on the head of their father. They did not have long claws on the ends of their fingers, and in appearance they were more like their mother; but in many ways they partook of the nature of both parents. They were strong and brave, like their father, but they had the wisdom of their grandfather, the Great Spirit. Thus the red man was created, for these were the first Indians.

With the passing of years the time came when the old mother grizzly knew she was soon to die; and, realizing that she had done wrong in keeping the child of the Great Spirit and never letting him know what had happened, she worried about this until she decided to do something to correct the wrong and ask forgiveness before her days on earth were ended. So she called all the grizzlies together at the big tepee which had been built for the princess and her family and told them what she had decided to do; and as soon as she had said these things she sent her son, who had married the princess, to the summit of Mount Shasta

11

to tell the Great Spirit where he could find his long-lost daughter.

The Great Spirit was so elated and so excited that he raced down the south side of the mountain, with such powerful strides that even to this day you can see the marks of his tracks. The grizzlies were all waiting for him. They stood in two great lines, with their clubs resting peacefully in their arms, and they made a lane through which the Great Spirit passed as in a tribal ceremony. He slowed his pace and walked with restrained emotion to where his daughter was waiting for him. But when he saw the children, and learned that the grizzlies had created a new race, he became very angry. It was only the Great Spirit's privilege to create new races of living things on the earth. His eyes flashed like the lightning as he stared at the old grizzly mother who had planned and been responsible for all this, and she immediately fell down and died on the spot. Seeing what the Great Spirit had done, all the other grizzlies became very incensed and, clutching their clubs in their right hands, they set up a loud howling of angry protest.

Becoming even more incensed at this, the Great Spirit took up his daughter and, holding her on his shoulder, his eyes flashed again. He ordered all the grizzlies to drop their clubs upon the ground, never again to use them, he forever silenced their voices, and he ordered them to get down on their hands and knees before him and so to remain until he released them from these orders. The grizzlies were unable to resist the will of the Great Spirit, and they all did as they were told.

Then he drove all of his daughter's children out into the world and bade them scatter in all the different directions, after which he tightly closed the door of the big tepee so they could not come back to live there. Then, carrying the fair one on his shoulder, he strode away, going back up the mountain. Never again did the Great Spirit return to the timber or release the bears from the orders which he had imposed upon them.

So it was that the Indians were created; and so it was that the grizzlies lost their power of speech and the use of clubs as weapons, and forever since they have had to walk about on four feet instead of two. Like other beasts they have had to use their claws and teeth as weapons, and only when they are compelled to fight for the preservation of their own honor or their lives does the Great Spirit permit them to stand up and walk like men.

This is how the Indians came to be. We know it happened this way because the story has come down to us, from father to son and from uncle to nephew, since the very beginning. That the grizzly once stood erect and walked like a man, one has but to look at them. Their arms are a great deal shorter than their legs; they walk flat-footed, and the soles of their feet are like your own. They have no tails and in all respects are more like man than any other animal. All this is why the old-time Indians about Mount Shasta would never kill or interfere in any way with a grizzly; for, if it were not for these bears, there would be no Indians today.

After this "great creation," Indians lived in relative harmony with nature — the grizzly included — for many decades. Then, the bear's and the Indian's nemesis, the white man, began to blaze a trail of change into the western wilderness.

Exactly what European first saw a grizzly will probably never be known. It could easily have been Cabeza de Vaca and three companions, as they were undoubtedly the first to challenge the grizzly's domain. They spent nine years — November, 1527, to July, 1536 — wandering through Texas and northern Mexico. Likewise, it could have been Francesco Vasquez de Coronado who crossed New Mexico, Colorado, Kansas, and Nebraska on a 1540-42 journey.

However, neither of these early explorers recorded any confrontation with the grizzly. But the thought of an armored Spanish conquistador with sword in hand squaring off against a half-ton plains grizzly conjures up vivid images.

In the northwest, a Frenchman, an early Jesuit missionary, Claude Jean Allouez, may have been the first to meet the grizzly. A 1666 entry in his journal tells of Indians who lived on raw fish and who "in turn are eaten by bears of frightful size, all red, and with prodigiously long claws." The editor of Allouez' journal, Dr. Louise Phelps Kellog, is convinced that these were grizzly bears in the Assiniboine River region west of Winnipeg, Manitoba. However, some argue Allouez didn't actually see the grizzly, but simply recorded the observations of native tribes. So most historians give credit for seeing the first grizzly to Henry Kelsey, a young Englishman employed by the Hudson Bay Company. The Historical and Scientific Society of Manitoba notes: "there can be no doubt whatever" that Kelsey was the first to "record a description" of the grizzly of Northwest Canada.

Kelsey's journal of "ye 20th August (1691)" reads: "To day we pitcht to ye outermost Edge of ye woods this plain affords Nothing but short Round sticky grass & Bullilo & a great sort of Bear wch is Bigger than any white Bear & is Neither White nor Black But silver hair'd...."

A semi-poetic September, 1691, entry reads:

13

And then you have beast of severall kind
The one is a black a Buffilo great
Another is an outgrown Bear wch. is good meat
His skin to gett I have used all ye ways I can
He is mans food & he makes food of man....

On May 14, 1804—113 years after Kelsey first described the grizzly in broken English—the memorable Lewis and Clark expedition left St. Louis. Many historians give Meriwether Lewis and William Clark credit for "discovering" the grizzly bear, although technically they weren't the first white men to see the grizzly. But undoubtedly they were the first to bring national attention to the grizzly and to collect the scientific (or "type") specimen from which early zoologists described and classified the species.

The expedition saw their first grizzly on October 20, 1804, near the mouth of the Heart River, North Dakota. From that point on, the explorers had dozens of confrontations with the awesome white bear. Often, the adventurers barely escaped with their lives. Using inadequate smooth bore rifles that shot round balls, the expedition found the grizzly most difficult to kill, as the account of May 5, 1805, illustrates.[1]

> ...it was a most tremendious looking anamal, and extreemly hard to kill notwithstanding he had five balls through his lungs and five others in various parts he swam more than half the distance across the river to a sandbar, & it was at least twenty minutes before he died; he did not attempt to attack, but fled and made the most tremendous roaring from the moment he was shot. We had no means of weighing this monster; Capt. Clark thought he would weigh 500 lbs. for my own part I think the estimate too small by 100 lbs. he measured 8. Feet 7½ Inches from the nose to the extremety of the hind feet, 5F. 10½ Ins. arround the breast, 1 F. 11.I. arround the middle of the arm, & 3 F. 11.I. arround the neck; his tallons which were five in number on each foot were 4⅜ Inches in length. he was in good order, we therefore divided him among the party and made them boil the oil and put it in a cask for future uce; the oil is as hard as hogs lard when cool, much more so than that of the black bear. this bear differs from the common black bear in several respects; it's tallons are much longer and more blont, it's tale shorter, it's hair which is of a redish or bey brown, is longer thicker and finer than that of the black bear; his liver lungs and heart are much larger even in proportion with

[1]From *The Journals of Lewis and Clark.* Edited by Bernard DeVoto. Houghton Mifflin Company, Boston, 1953.

his size; the heart particularly was as large as that of a large Ox. his maw was also ten times the size of black bear, and was filled with flesh and fish.

The big bears were apparently numerous around the present-day city of Great Falls, Montana. Here, the two captains forbade their crew to leave camp at night for fear of the grizzlies. While in this vicinity, the expedition killed 10 grizzlies.

The expedition was forced to spend extra time in this area because of the difficulty of portaging around a series of five spectacular falls on the Missouri River, perhaps one of the early West's most scenic and historic sites. Regrettably, the Montana Power Company later turned the area into a series of reservoirs, completely inundating the falls.

Lewis theorized that the unusually large grizzly population was, in part, due to the number of buffalo which inadvertently were washed over the falls while they were swimming the river. He observed that bears fed on the mangled carcasses.

On the way West, the expedition saw their last silvertip along the Jefferson River, near Waterloo, Montana, on August 1, 1805. They didn't see another grizzly west of that point. In short, they traveled from a point about 100 miles east of the Continental Divide all the way to the West Coast without seeing another grizzly. On the way back, they killed six grizzlies in the Clearwater Valley, near Kamiah, Idaho.

In his book, *The Natural History Of The Lewis & Clark Expedition*, Raymond Darwin Burroughs compiled a list of game killed by the explorers. Incredibly, they shot at least 43 grizzlies. Today, students of Lewis and Clark like Ken Walcheck of the Montana Department of Fish and Game ask, "Why were so many grizzlies killed? For what purpose? Surely, not for food, as one can find little evidence in the journals of explorers eating bear meat. And it remains extremely doubtful all the bears were rendered for bear oil.

"It also remains extremely doubtful the explorers killed all of the grizzlies in actual 'showdown' confrontations," Walcheck explains. "One has to question whether Lewis was really sincere in his statement, 'although' game is very abundant and gentle, we only kill as much as is necessary for food."[1]

With this background, one can hardly avoid thinking the great white bear represented an ultra-tempting challenge for early hunters. Perhaps it was the beginning of a destined-to-continue contest to see who would rule the

[1]Walcheck, Ken. "Lewis and Clark Meet the Awesome White Bear." *Montana Outdoors*. September-October 1976. Vol. 7. No. 5. p. 42.

West—white man or white bear. The great bear had ruled the plains Indians with their frail wooden weapons, but the white man, with his rifles, was too much for the grizzly back in 1805-6 and from then on.

"As the Lewis and Clark encounters with the great white bear were told, revised and revitalized over a thousand campfires, the ferocity of the grizzly grew in direct proportion to the number of times the tales were told," Walcheck explains. "Encounters with grizzlies by later explorers added more zing and zest to the tales and in short order Old Ephraim gained a sinister reputation surpassing that of any other North American carnivore. Writers, armed with active pens and artists with energetic paintbrushes, portrayed the grizzly as a killer — an unsavory quadruped to avoid at all costs. Unfortunately, the grizzly's true character has seldom been depicted in its proper perspective."

One can only wonder about, not criticize, the adverse relationship between the expedition and the great bear, however. Lewis and Clark made a marvelous contribution to science with their detailed natural history references, of which the grizzly is a particularly good example. In fact, Elliott Coues, an editor of the original journals, stated in a footnote that the grizzly was the most notable zoological discovery made by Lewis and Clark.

After their journals became popular around 1825, the world soon knew the grizzly as North America's most fierce beast. Quickly, the writings of early mountain men and other explorers began to circulate, many accounts containing flashy references to the grizzly. Through most of this early literature, including the Lewis and Clark journals, ran a common undertone. This bear was a threat to man, a magnificent menace which was slain without thought of the future. Since grizzlies were in such abundance and the wilderness so vast, what early explorer could conceive the grizzly's future desperation? Old Ephraim's fierce image became entrenched, much to his misfortune, as the grizzly population started to dwindle.

In the following decades, mountain men and early trappers roamed the West. These wiry, wilderness-wise wanderers were a rare breed indeed, living for many months off nature. Their day-by-day experiences — killing a grizzly with a hunting knife, enduring the western winter, eluding hostile Indians, would undoubtedly grip readers today. Unfortunately, most of these adventurers went to their graves without recording a single word for future generations to relish. A few — Jedediah Smith, Jim Bridger, Joe Meek, Kit Carson, James Capen Adams ("Grizzly Adams"), Ben Lilly, High Glass, and others like them — have their place in history, but many died unknown.

16

These early pathfinders waged war on the wilderness king. Killing grizzlies was even an obsession to some, perhaps a continuous contest to see who would rule the mountains. However, even though this first troop of hunters "undid" many grizzlies, bear numbers remained relatively high in many areas, but not in California, which probably hosted the greatest original concentrations of grizzlies anywhere.

California's abundant "golden bears" (still pictured on the state flag) faced a new dilemma. The Spanish culture dominating California in the early 1800s created a new dimension to the homeland tradition of bullfights and cockfights — a fight to the death between bull and bear. No book on the grizzly can omit an account of these incredible bull/bear battles.

Bears were plentiful, but capturing a live grizzly — and particularly a large California bruin — was no trivial task. Also, the bigger and more ferocious the bear was, the better. Finding, lassoing, hog-tying, and transporting these brutes thus became the sport of sports among the courageous *vaqueros* of Old California.

First, the bear was driven into the open. Quickly, lasso after lasso encircled the bear's neck and legs until the bruin was tightly suspended between at least four horsemen. A brave soul then crept in to tie the heavy paws together. This usually enraged the roped bear, but somehow all four legs were hog-tied. The grizzly was then muzzled and transported to an arena for a bloody battle with a big bull.

Before the rush of gold-seekers to California, the bear/bull battles usually highlighted some festive holiday. After the state filled with miners, gamblers and promoters, though, the fights were staged strictly for profit. The excitement-starved, whiskey-filled gold miners paid handsomely for the pleasure of seeing a bear and bull kill each other.

In the center of the arena, the bear was usually secured to a post with a 15-25 foot chain shackled to a back leg. Different promoters had different ideas about their show. But in most cases, bulls were turned loose to attack the bear, one at a time, each additional one costing the crowd more, until a sharp bovine horn found its way into the bruin's chest. Some of the famous fighting grizzlies tore apart five or six bulls in a single afternoon's performance. Promoters often saved their fighting bears for another Sunday festival and another fat profit.

In a dramatic and gruesome description, Major Horace Bell described this early California bear/bullfight.[1]

[1]Bartlett, Lanier, Ed. *Major Horace Bell: On The Old West Coast.* William Morrow and Company, Publishers, Inc. New York. 1930.

In the great fiestas of times past at the Missions and Presidios there was always a bull and bear fight for the entertainment of the crowd. The last one on record that I know of took place at Pala, a branch of *asistencia* at the once great Mission San Luis Rey, in the mountains of San Diego County; nearly fifty years ago. One of the American newspapers in California published an account of it written by a correspondent who was present. I have the clipping of that and as it is a better-written description than I could produce myself, I give it herewith:

The bear was an ugly grizzly that for years had roamed the pine-clad region of Palomar Mountain, rising six thousand feet above the little Mission. Tied to a huge post in the center of the old adobe-walled quadrangle he stood almost as high as a horse, a picture of fury such as painter never conceived. His hind feet were tethered with several turns of a strong rawhide reata, but were left about a yard apart to give full play. To the center of this rawhide, between the two feet, was fastened another heavy reata, doubled and secured to a big loop made of doubled reatas thrown over the center post. The services of a man on horseback with a long pole were constantly needed to keep the raging monster from chewing through the rawhide ropes.

By the time the bear had stormed around long enough to get well limbered up after being tied all night the signal was given, the horseman effected his disappearance and in dashed a bull through an open gate. He was of the old long-horn breed but of great weight and power. He had been roaming the hills all summer, living like a deer in the chaparral of the rough mountains and was as quick and wild as any deer. He, too, like old bruin, had been captured with the noosed lazo in a sudden dash of horsemen on a little flat he crossed to go to a spring at daylight and felt no more in love with mankind than did the bear. As he dashed across the arena it looked as if the fight was going to be an unequal one, but the bear gave a glance that intimated that no one need waste sympathy on him.

No creature is so ready for immediate business as is the bull turned loose in an amphitheater of human faces. He seems to know they are there to see him fight and he wants them to get their money's worth. So, as soon as the gate admits him, he goes for everything in sight with the dash of a cyclone. Things that outside he would fly from or not notice he darts at as eagerly as a terrier for a rat the instant he sees them in the ring.

This bull came from the same mountains as the bear and they were old acquaintances, though the acquaintance had been cultivated on the run as the bull tore with thundering hoofs through the tough manzanita or went plunging down the steep hillside as the evening breeze wafted

18

the strong scent of the bear to his keen nose. But now, in the arena, he spent no time looking for a way of escape but at a pace that seemed impossible for even the great weight of the bear to resist he rushed across the ring directly at the enemy as if he had been looking for him all his life.

With wonderful quickness for so large an animal the bear rose on his hind legs and cooly waited until the long sharp horns were within a yard of his breast. Then up went the great paws, one on each side of the bull's head, and the sharp points of the horns whirled up from horizontal to perpendicular, then almost to horizontal again as bull and bear went rolling over together. In a twinkling the bear was on his feet again, but the bull lay limp as a rag, his neck broken.

In rode four horsemen and threw reatas around the feet of the dead bull, while the grizzly did his ferocious best to get at them. As they dragged the body of the vanquished victim out one gate, the runway to the bullpen was opened once more and a second bull, a big black one with tail up as if to switch the moon, charged into the arena. On his head glistened horns so long and sharp that it seemed impossible for the bear ever to reach the head with his death-dealing paws before being impaled.

But this problem did not seem to worry the grizzly. He had not been living on cattle for so many years without knowing a lot about their movements. When this new antagonist came at him he dodged as easily as a trained human bullfighter, and as the bull shot past him down came one big paw on the bovine's neck with a whack that sounded all over the adobe corral. A chorus of shouts went up from the rows of swarthy faces, with here and there a white face, as the victim, turning partly over, went down with a plunge that made one of his horns plow up dirt, then break sharp off under the terrific pressure of his weight and momentum.

The bull was not done for; he tried to rise and bruin made a dash for him, but his tethers held him short of his goal. In a second the bull got to his feet and wheeled around with one of those short twists that makes him so dangerous an antagonist. But once he is wheeled around his course is generally straight ahead and a quick dodger can avoid him; however, he is lightening-like in his charge and something or somebody is likely to be overhauled in short order. So it was this time and before the bear could recover from the confusion into which he had been thrown by being brought up short by his tether, the bull caught him on the shoulder with his remaining horn.

Few things in nature are tougher than the shoulder of a grizzly bear and a mere side swing without the full weight of a running bull behind it was insufficient to make even this sharp horn penetrate. The bear

19

staggered, but the horn glanced from the ponderous bone, leaving a long gash in the shaggy hide. This only angered bruin the more. He made a grab for the head of the bull but again was frustrated by the reatas which allowed him only a limited scope of action.

The bull returned to the charge as soon as he could turn himself around and aimed the long horn full at his enemy's breast. But just as the horn seemed reaching its mark the grizzly grabbed the bull's head with both paws and twisted it half round, with the nose inward. The nose he seized in his great white teeth and over both went in a swirl of dust while the crowd roared and cheered.

Now one could see exactly why cattle found killed by bears always have their necks broken. Bears do not go through the slow process of strangling or bleeding their victims, but do business on scientific principles.

This time the grizzly rose more slowly than before, nevertheless he rose, while the bull lay still in death.

The owners of the bear now wanted to stop the show but from all sides rose a roar of "Otro! Otro! Otro! Otro toro!" "Another! Another! Another! Another bull!"

The owners protested that the bear was disabled and was too valuable to sacrifice needlessly; that a dead bull was worth as much as a live one, and more, but that the same arithmetic did not hold good for a bear. The clamor of the crowd grew minute by minute, for the sight of blood gushing from the bear's shoulder was too much for the equilibrium of an audience like this one.

Soon another bull shot toward the center of the arena. Larger than the rest but thinner, more rangy, he opened negotiations with even more vigor, more speed. With thundering thump of great hoofs, his head wagging from side to side, eyes flashing green fire, he drove full at the bear with all his force. The grizzly was a trifle clumsy this time and as he rose to his hind feet the bull gave a twist of his head that upset the calculations of the bear. Right into the base of the latter's neck went a long sharp horn, at the same time that the two powerful paws closed on the bull's neck from above. A distinct crack was heard. The bull sank forward carrying the bear over backward with a heavy thump against the big post to which he was tied.

Again the horsemen rode in to drag out a dead bull. But the grizzly now looked weary and pained. Another pow-wow with his owners ensued while the crowd yelled more loudly than ever for another bull. The owners protested that it was unfair, but the racket rose louder and louder for the audience knew that there was one bull left, the biggest and wildest of the lot.

The crowd won, but bruin was given a little more room in which to fight. Vaqueros rode in and while two lassoed his forepaws and spread him out in front, the other two looosened his ropes behind so as to give him more play. He now had about half the length of a reata. Allowing him a breathing spell, which he spent trying to bite off the reatas, the gate of the bullpen was again thrown open.

Out dashed an old Red Rover of the hills and the way he went for the bear seemed to prove him another old acquaintance. He seemed anxious to make up for the many times he had flown from the distant scent that had warned him that the bear was in the same mountains. With lowered head turned to one side so as to aim one horn at the enemy's breast he cleared the distance in half a dozen leaps.

The bear was still slower than before in getting to his hind feet and his right paw slipped as he grabbed the bull's head. He failed to twist it over. The horn struck him near the base of the neck and bull and bear went rolling over together.

Loud cheers for the bull rose as the bear, scrambling to his feet, showed blood coming from a hole in his neck almost beside the first wound. Still louder roared the applause as the bull regained his feet. Lashing his sides with his tail and bounding high in fury he wheeled and returned to the fray. The bear rolled himself over like a ball and would have been on his feet again safely had not one foot caught in the reata which tied him to the post. Unable to meet the bull's charge with both hind feet solid on the ground he fell forward against his antagonist and received one horn full in the brest, up to the hilt.

But a great grizzly keeps on fighting even after a thrust to the heart. Again he struggled to his feet, the blood gushing from the new wound. With stunning quickness in so large an animal the bull had withdrawn his horn, gathered himself together and returned to the charge. The bear could not turn in time to meet him and with a heavy smash the horn struck him squarely in the shoulder forward of the protecting bone. Those who have seen the longest horns driven full to the hilt through the shoulder of a horse — a common sight in the bull-fights of Mexico — can understand why the bear rolled over backward to rise no more.

Long before the last cheers came from the California arenas (1855-65), the grizzly had met his match over most of his domain. The livestock industry did more to exterminate the grizzly from 90% of his habitat than any other single force.

"The most potential contributing factor in the destruction of the grizzly in the United States," writes Harold McCracken in his 1955 book *The Beast That Walks Like a Man*, "was the introduction of domestic cattle and farm stock into the grassy mountain valleys and more open ranges west of the Great Plains.

"Everyone became aware of the stock-killing activities of the big bears, and the new interest in cattle as a remunerative enterprise put a new emphasis on the bear situation. The problem was taken so seriously in some areas that the ranchers combined their efforts and carried out an organized campaign to exterminate the ursine vandals. Thus, the grizzly became marked as the first and foremost predatory enemy of the cattlemen — an unfortunate imputation which was destined to follow the stock industry as closely as the lariat and the branding iron and to survive as long as there was a grizzly left in the country."

One can draw a near-perfect parallel between the dwindling native tribes and the disappearing grizzly. The pioneers first wiped out the bison and then turned over the rich sod, more-or-less eliminating the plains grizzly and the plains Indian, both of which depended on the vast bison herds for subsistence.

With native Americans, bears, and bison vanishing, the livestock industry spread across the grass oceans like a tidal wave. The frontier "Indian fighters" and cavalry coined the creed, "The only good Injun is a dead Injun;" and the cattle barons and sheepmen followed with, "The only good grizzly is a dead grizzly."

Vernon Bailey, in *Mammals of New Mexico*, a 1931 volume, wrote: "The destruction of these grizzlies is absolutely necessary before the stock business in the region could be maintained on a profitable basis." And stockmen's organizations heartily agreed.

Some grizzlies did prey on stock, but how much stock was killed and whether this loss warranted wholesale extermination of bears are debatable. Enos Mills, a confessed grizzly lover and author of a 1919 book on the big bear, claimed only 1 out of every 100 grizzlies ever killed stock. Apparently, that was too many.

Many grizzlies were wrongly accused, just as many eagles were falsely blamed in the early 1970s for sheep predation. Carrion-loving grizzlies fed on cattle and sheep already dead from other causes. In this manner, some bears no doubt cultivated a taste for beef and mutton, which led to future stock-killing. The most famous grizzlies of the old West — Old Mose, Old Ephraim, Old Timberline, Old Big Foot, Old Club Foot, Bloody Paws, Three Toes, Old Silver, The Phantom, The Crippler, Slaughterhouse, Red Robber, El Tejon, White Face, and more—were the confirmed stock-killers. A few of these big brutes even killed some glory-seeking bounty hunters.

Poison baits, large bounties, new repeating rifles, packs of trained hunting dogs, and set guns all went into the war between man and grizzly. Furthermore, "government trappers" from the federal government helped, since many sheep and cows grazed on public land. Together, the bounty hunters, stockmen, and government trappers searched everywhere for Old Ephraim. When they found him, they killed him.

Interestingly, the livestock industry didn't seem agitated over the grizzly's poor cousin, the black bear. Stockmen hated all predators, but their hatred focused on the "summit" species, such as the grizzly. The grizzly, wolf, and mountain lion were the hardened criminals; the black bear, coyote, and bobcat were the juvenile delinquents.

Through the early 1900s, the war raged. The great bear was banished to the most secluded retreats, where he clung to an uncertain future. Perhaps his great intelligence, his ability to quickly cope with man's objectives, was Old Ephraim's temporary salvation.

Old Ephraim's grave in northern Utah. Although Old Ephraim was a local name for an individual stock-killing grizzly, the name was later applied to the grizzly bear as a species. Hopefully, this epitaph doesn't foretell the future of all grizzly bears. Photo courtesy of the Utah Division of Wildlife.

Chapter 3

THE
PASSING
OF OLD EPHRAIM

Hounded, hunted, and harassed, "the horrible bear" of the western wilderness steadily gave ground. First, explorers and mountain men came. Then, trappers, stockmen, homesteaders, miners, and all the rest moved in.

The plains grizzly went first—his primary food source, the bison, destroyed and his territory, the native sod, lying upside down. Soon, mountain range after mountain range became bearless. State after state saw the last specimen of its most magnificent mammal nailed on a barn door. Some states even failed to document the loss. Undoubtedly, the grizzly's plight typifies the early American's insensitivity toward wild creatures and natural systems during his blitz to conquer the great wilderness.

Historical records are spotty and, at times, suspect, but extensive research has revealed the following details on the passing of Old Ephraim.

Strangely, Nevada has no record of the big bear, even though surrounding states supported large populations. The Nevada Department of Fish and Game says the grizzly "never existed" in that state. Likewise, no other source verified the past existence of the grizzly in Nevada.

**Grizzly Country
1800**

Kansas, Oklahoma, and Nebraska have scanty or no records — although the plains grizzly most likely frequented these states along with the "infinite" bison herds.

E.L. Cockrum, in his book, *Mammals of Kansas,* notes, "Although few records remain, the grizzly bear probably formerly roamed over most of the western two-thirds of the state. Almost nothing of the occurrence and habits of this bear in Kansas has been recorded in literature."

Oklahoma and Nebraska have even less to offer history. But it's almost certain that Old Ephraim lived there. Regretfully, his presence passed into oblivion undocumented.

Texas at least has an official record of the state's last grizzly. One October, in 1890, C.O. Finley and John Z. Means were riding the range in the Davis Mountains of western Texas. In a gulch near the head of Limpia Creek, they found where a bear had killed a cow and eaten most of it. Shortly thereafter, they returned with a pack of 52 hounds to track down and finish the stock killer. Out of the large pack, only a few of the hounds would follow the trail, even though they were all accustomed to hunting black bear, and even those few followed the trail reluctantly.

After a five-mile run through rough country, the dogs brought the bear to bay. The bear killed one hound before the rifles of Finley and Means quieted Texas' last recorded grizzly.

It took four men to hoist the skin (with head and feet attached) onto a horse for the return to camp. Finley estimated the weight of the bear at about 1,100 pounds — "if it had been fat." Vernon Bailey noted in his book *Biological Survey of Texas.* that this bear was indeed a very old male grizzly.

The Dakotas come next. Both states entered the 20th Century without grizzlies, but again, documentation is sparse.

Several early authors mentioned grizzlies in the Black Hills of western South Dakota. However, no official record of the last South Dakota silvertip

**Grizzly Country
1900**

can be found.

Early naturalists also observed grizzlies in North Dakota — especially along the Little Missouri River in the southwestern part of the state, near where Theodore Roosevelt ranched, and in the Devil's Lake/Sheyenne River country in eastern North Dakota. The last official report recorded two grizzlies killed by Dave Warren near Oakdale in 1897.

Of all the states where the grizzly once ranged, California has left the best testimony of the passing. Judging from the many historical accounts, California had, at the least, a large grizzly population — perhaps more bears than any other state. Now the "golden bear lives only on the state's flag. Most sources claim Jesse B. Agnew shot the last grizzly near his cattle ranch at Horse Corral Meadow, Tulare County, in 1922.

However, there are a few historical hints that the "golden bear" haunted California for a few more years. For example, several qualified observers reported a grizzly in the Sequoia National Park vicinity until 1924. Nevertheless, California repeats the story of other states — extermination.

Old Ephraim *really* died in Utah, as witnessed by the picture on page 24. The life and death of Old Ephraim, a famous stock-killing grizzly, has been immortalized in northern Utah. Because Frank Clark, a Utah sheepherder responsible for this old bear's undoing, was dissatisfied with the publicity the incident received, he wrote the following article for the *Utah Wildlife Bulletin,* the former publication of the Utah Department of Fish and Game.

> I was transferred to the Cache National Forest from Idaho in 1911. This country was infested with bears at that time. They were of two varieties: the brown and the grizzly bear. Many of them were sheep killers. I know of them killing as many as 150 head of sheep in one summer from one herd.
>
> The men were not used to these killer bears and I had some trouble trying to get men to stay on the job. After we had killed and trapped one or two, however, their feelings toward them changed. I killed 13 in 1912 alone.
>
> One bear had become known as Old Ephraim. He was a grizzly bear. The bear's name was given to him, I think, because of an outlaw bear found in California that had been written up by P.S. Barnham. Old Ephraim was well known, mainly because everyone who saw his tracks recognized him. He had one deformed toe. Many weird tales were told about him. He was supposed to have ranged all the way from northern Utah to the Snake River section in Idaho, but I never found his tracks more than two miles from the range that I was using.
>
> I began in 1914 to trap for him, but it was not until 1923 that I caught

28

him. He had a large pool scooped out in a little canyon and at least once a week he would come to wallow in the pool he had made. I set my trap in this pool thinking I would catch him, but every time I set it and the bear visited the pool, he would "pertly" pick it up and set it on the side of the pool. It was not until 1923 that he changed his plan of enjoying himself in this wallow. I thought of moving the trap each time. One time I came back and found the bear had dug another pool just below the old one. I set my trap in the new location and this proved Old Ephraim's undoing.

Old Ephraim was not the greedy killer that some bears seem to be. He would usually kill one sheep, pick it up and carry it into the more remote sections of the mountains and devour it. This is in strict contrast to the actions of some killer bears who may kill as many as 100 sheep in one night. It had become a legend that Old Ephraim never seemed to pick on the same herd twice in succession, but roamed around for several miles, in the proximity of the spring where he bathed and would take only one or two sheep from each separate camp.

I remember well the night of Old Ephraim's undoing. I had set the trap in his new pool, stirred up the mud so that it would set well on the trap. My camp was about one mile down stream from the site. April 23 was a beautiful cool night and after supper I lighted my pipe and set my gaze at the stars that seemed to be trying to get a message of some kind to the people down here. My nearest company were other herders about four miles away and my horses on a meadow some distance below my camp.

After bedding down for the night and sleeping for some time I was suddenly awakened by the most unearthly sound I have ever heard. Ordinarily my dog would bark at anything unusual; this time he did not. After the first cry, I noticed that the grumbling of this bear stopped and then after a short time, a roar heard again, echoed from canyon wall to canyon wall. I quickly slipped on my shoes, didn't bother to put on pants, grabbed my rifle and started along the trail. Expecting to go only a few yards from camp, qas why I did not fully dress. As the sounds kept up I could tell they were in the bottom of the canyon nearing me. I skirted the mountain side above. I finally realized that I had caught either Old Ephraim or another bear and soon heard the noise in the willows along the creek bed below me. After it had passed, I slipped down and along the trail in the bright moon light and I could see the tracks of the big bear as he went down the stream. I followed the noise slowly down the creek until I got near the point where my camp was and there came crashing out of the creek bottom the giant form of Old Ephraim walking on his hind feet. He was carrying on his front foot the

29

large trap that weighed 27 pounds and the 15 feet of log chain neatly wrapped around his right forearm. As he cmcame towards me, it chilled me to the very bone and for several paces I didn't even attempt to shoot. Finally, more out of fear than any other passion, I opened up with my small 25-35 caliber rifle and pumped six shots into him. He fell at my feet dead, and as I looked at the giant form of Old Ephraim I suddenly became sorry that I had killed this giant bear. Retracing the bear's trail from the place where he had been caught I found that for over one mile he had walked on his hind feet holding the trap and chain on his front foot. Also, that he had cut the large 15 foot log that I had the chain tied to in 2 and 3 foot lengths. All the trees as far as the length of the chain would let him go had been cut down. It looked as if the quaking aspen up to six inches in diameter had been cut with a single blow.

Old Ephraim's body was buried near my camp site and remained there until it was unearthed and his skull sent to the Smithsonian Institute where it remains today. A monument has been erected by the Boy Scouts of America of Cache County to the memory of Old Ephraim and hundreds of Boy Scouts have visited my camp and been thrilled to the story I have told hundreds of times of the killing of Old Ephraim.

In 1917, an official survey estimated the New Mexico grizzly population at 48. In 1927, the same surveyors reported the species had reached the point of "almost total extermination." An article published in the October 1961 issue of *Arizona Wildlife-Sportsman,* states the "last kill" came in 1933.

Hunting in the Jemez Mountains, Tom Campbell shot the state's last grizzly in the stomach, and it ran away. But Campbell found it dead three days later at the head of Santa Clara Canyon — evidence of the slow, agonizing end of Old Ephraim in New Mexico.

The U.S. Fish and Wildlife Service claims Richard R. Miller killed the last Arizona grizzly, in Greenlee County, in 1935. The same issue of *Arizona Wildlife-Sportsman* carries this account of the last Arizona grizzly:

The day the last grizzly reported to be killed in Arizona was no different than any other on the Joe Filleman spread near Red Mt. northeast of Clifton. Dick had his 30-30 in the scabbard under his left leg and was riding his pet hunting horse. His seven hounds were along as Dick went out that day looking for a calf kill. He was in the bottom of Stray Horse Canyon, east of Rose Peak, when the dogs lit out on a bear scent. In a matter of minutes, they doubled back and came in under him. Dick fired from the saddle and killed the bear running in front of the

30

pack. It was a two year old and Miller estimated it to weigh about 200 pounds. He looked around the area and found evidence that the two year old had a twin and a mother in the area. It was late, so Dick skinned the bear and headed for the ranch.

A couple of days later, Kit Casto and Mr. Black rode in. Dick mentioned the kill and showed the men the skin nailed on a log. Both men immediately identified the bear as a grizzly.

Dick Miller told this writer that he would have never killed the bear had he known it was a grizzly. The other two grizzlies were never seen again. The date of the last recorded grizzly kill in Arizona was September 13, 1935.

In *A Sand County Almanac,* Aldo Leopold describes one of Arizona's greatest grizzlies and how he passed away. This bear wasn't the last, but rather one of the last. Certainly the plight of Old Bigfoot typifies the West's attitude toward the grizzly.

Old Bigfoot lived on Escudilla, a famous mountain in the Apache National Forest. "There was, in fact, only one place from which you did not see Escudilla on the skyline; that was the top of Escudilla itself," Leopold wrote. "Up there you could not see the mountain, but you could feel it. The reason was the big bear."

Old Bigfoot crawled out of his den each spring, descended the mountain, and bashed in the head of one cow. After eating his fill, he climbed back into the crags and stayed there all summer, no longer bothering the cattle herds. "I once saw one of his kills," Leopold noted. "The cow's skull and neck were pulp, as if she had collided head-on with a fast freight."

Old Bigfoot claimed only one cow a year. But that was too many. Leopold wrote how progress — automobiles, telephones, electric power, and other "necessities" of modern men — began coming to cow country. "One spring, progress sent still another emissary, a government trapper, a sort of St. George in overalls, seeking dragons to slay at government expense. Were there, he asked, any destructive animals in need of slaying? Yes, there was a big bear."

The government trapper tried everything — traps, poison, and all his usual wiles. But Old Bigfoot was too wise. Then, the trapper erected a set-gun, and, as Leopold put it, "The last grizzly walked into the string and shot himself."

"Escudilla still hangs on the horizon," Leopold remorsefully explains, "but when you see it you no longer think of bear. It's only a mountain now."

And this carnage continued to spread. Oregon was next. According to the

31

Oregon Wildlife Commission, the last Oregon grizzly was killed by Evans Stoneman, a government trapper, on Chesnimnus Creek, in Wallowa County on September 14, 1931. Reports of grizzlies continued until 1940, but none have been verified.

Manitoba lost its grizzlies along with the bison, but the Canadian Wildlife Service doesn't have a date for the bear's demise. The best estimate Manitoba wildlife officials can offer is "about 150 years ago."

Grizzly Country 1950

Colorado was the last in a long list of states to wipe out the wilderness king. Checking around for the exact date of the last kill stirred up an ironic debate.

First, a letter from a retired government trapper, Ernest Wilkinson, claims the last Colorado silvertip. "As far as I know," Wilkinson wrote, "I took the last Grizzly Bear taken in Colorado in September, 1951 on Starvation Gulch in the Upper Rio Grande River Country."

Later, another retired government trapper, Floyd Anderson, wrote and said he killed the last one in 1952. Adding credence to this later record, the Colorado Division of Wildlife lists Anderson's bear as the last grizzly killed in the state.

Anderson, however, feels there are still a few grizzlies in the Continental Divide area between the Rio Grande and San Juan drainages in south central Colorado. "We know they're there," Anderson assures. "But it's difficult to prove." The retired trapper recalls tracking a grizzly for several miles in 1957, and his hunting dogs chased another one for 12 hours in 1964. He also tells of watching a female with two cubs for 20 minutes in 1967.

Richard Denny of the Division of Wildlife sides with Anderson, noting especially the sighting of a female with cubs in 1967. "Later unverified, or less creditable, observations have been made — through the 1960s and as late as 1973," Denny comments.

Smokey Till, also speaking for the Division of Wildlife, is less optimistic. "I don't think so," he says. "As many hunters as we have in there each fall,

**Grizzly Country
1975**

33

we'd know it."

Has the Colorado grizzly vanished? Most likely. But even if a few stragglers are hanging on, their numbers must be too low to constitute a viable population. Thus, their passing is fated.

It's pleasant to think that Colorado still supports a few grizzlies. But such thinking is more like dreaming.

Approximately 175 years of progress have been just about all Old Ephraim can take. Today, his home has shrunk to a small fraction of its original vastness. In the lower 48 states, only small portions of Idaho, Montana, Washington, and Wyoming have saved some wild country for the great bear.

The silvertip clings to most of his original range in British Columbia, reports D.R. Halladay of the British Columbia Fish and Wildlife Branch. "But its numbers are greatly reduced near human settlement, particularly in southern valleys."

Alberta, like Manitoba, lost its plains grizzlies early. However, the big bear hung on in the western mountains along the Continental Divide and in the Swan Hills, south of Lesser Slave Lake.

The grizzly also inhabits all of the Yukon Territory and the mountains west of the Mackenzie River in the Northwest Territory. The barren ground grizzly, a distinct subspecies, still exists in low numbers east of Hudson Bay.

Mexico may have a few grizzlies in the rugged Baranca country along the Sonora-Chihauhua border in the head of Yaqui Basin, according to Dr. A. Starker Leopold, a noted bear authority from the University of California, Berkeley. Information on Mexico's last recorded kill isn't available. But Dr. Leopold has this bad news: "The small remnant that I found in the 1950s...has apparently been poisoned out of the Sierra del Nido Chihuahua. A local rancher had trouble with a bear killing livestock and got a hold of a batch of 1080 poison which he used rather generously. We have no recent reports of grizzlies in that area."

Of all the states and provinces, Alaska has the brightest news. "No one knows how many brown and grizzly bears Alaska has," Jim Rearden, of the Alaska Board of Game reports. "There is, however, substantial agreement that the population is the highest it has been in years, and it is still increasing in the interior, on the Kenai Peninsula, and in some other areas. Some estimate 15,000 or more."

The last reported grizzly killed in Washington was in 1964, but the big bear still survives near the Canada border. "Each year our personnel receive reports of grizzly tracks or grizzly sightings in northern Pend Oreille

County...," J. Burton Lauckhart, former game division chief with the Washington Department of Game, writes. "This is a small extension of the Selkirk Mountains (which lie mostly in British Columbia) that provides good grizzly habitat. The other area that still supports a small nucleus of grizzlies is the North Cascades area that is now in the new National Park."

"We carry an estimate of ten grizzlies in Washington, but this is only a guess to cover two or three family groups," Lauckhart admits.

Management in Washington now includes total protection from hunting. However, the game department notes, "If a stray animal does move into farming areas, it would have to be eliminated."

Jim Humbird, formerly of the Idaho Fish and Game Department, feels Idaho has more grizzly habitat than any other state, excluding Alaska. Yet, Idaho's grizzly population has steadily declined — even though hunting was banned in 1946. In the million-acre Selway/Bitterroot Wilderness on the Idaho/Montana border, for example, the last grizzly may have recently disappeared. The U.S. Fish and Wildlife Service still lists the grizzly as "threatened" in the Selway/Bitterroot; however, reports have been so sparse and suspect lately that many authorities fear the bear's extinction. Dr. Maurice Hornocker, leader of the Idaho Cooperative Wildlife Research Unit, suspects this, as does Dr. John Craighead. But there is no firm proof, or as Hornocker notes, "There may still be a few stragglers left."

Idaho still has grizzlies, most of which range in the Targhee National Forest on the west edge of Yellowstone Park. The northernmost part of the panhandle also has a few. But one of the largest expanse of primitive land remaining intact south of Canada — the 2.3 million-acre proposed River of No Return Wilderness in central Idaho — is without grizzlies.

That leaves Montana and Wyoming. These two states shelter the vast majority of the lower 48's last grizzlies. Neither state likes to estimate the population. However, most authorities will accept a "guess" of "less than 1,000" south of Canada.

Most of Wyoming's share of this remnant population inhabits the Shoshone and Teton national forests, east and south of Yellowstone Park, and the park itself.

Montana has the largest grizzly population in the lower 48 states. The Gallatin, Beaverhead, and Custer national forests, north and west of Yellowstone Park, support a struggling population. And northwestern Montana — Glacier Park, the Blackfoot and Flathead Indian reservations and the Flathead, Lewis and Clark, Kootenai, Helena, and Lolo national forests — probably hold more grizzlies than any other area south of the Canadian border.

It's in these few enclaves scattered around the northern Rockies, and particularly Montana and Wyoming, where Old Ephraim will make his last stand.

For ages, Old Ephraim roamed where he pleased with a robust defiance of all other animals, fearing nothing — including the native tribes. Then, his nemesis, the white man, spread over the west like a deadly disease, striking quickly, efficiently, and unemotionally.

Even with most of his kingdom gone, Old Ephraim asked for little — only to be left to himself in a few remote retreats. But the West's early residents wouldn't leave the bear alone. Employing every destructive tool they could conceive, they searched each mountain cirque for the beleaguered bear. And they felt little emotion when skinning each state's last grizzly — except a sense of pride for relieving the livestock industry of a serious menace.

Considering the war-like campaign to rid the West of Old Ephraim, it's remarkable that he has survived at all. Indeed, a lesser animal would have perished. But the wilderness king never lost his wit, his fierce tenacity for life, or his savage dignity. For centuries he had ruled unchallenged, until he met his match. Then sensing that his only salvation lay in retreat, he adapted and fled. Somehow, Old Ephraim survived to carry his majestic race into the 1970s.

In his article, "Vanished Monarch of the Sierra," published in the May/June 1976 issue of *The American West*, Ted M. Taylor came up with an appropriate closing for a detailed description of the disappearance of the big bear.

"In 1868, Bret Harte, editor of the *Overland Monthly*, explained the meaning of the publication's symbol — a grizzly crossing railroad tracks," Taylor wrote. "After noting that the railroad, representing civilization, foretold the bear's doom, Harte wrote of the California grizzly: 'Look at him well, for he is passing away. Fifty years and he will be as extinct as the dodo....'

"Today grizzlies still may be found in considerable numbers in Alaska and Canada, and a few are even said to survive in portions of Sonora, Mexico," Taylor noted. "But in the western United States, once home of some 100,000 such animals, a dwindling remnant of fewer than 1,000 grizzlies remains, most in remote sections of the Rocky Mountain region. Look at them well...."

Chapter 4

THE
GRIZZLY
STORY

Americans finally woke up — unhappy to see a vital part of their heritage slipping away. After 175 years of hating and persecuting the bear, they were suddenly seeking his salvation.

Too often, important issues lack ample public interest to encourage adequate protective measures. Although public apathy is the nation's number one conservation problem, fortunately, it doesn't play a major role in efforts to preserve the grizzly. Americans want the big bear around forever. And at times, they don't mind getting vocal about it. There may even be enough public concern for the grizzly to force appropriate action — if only the pressure can be directed to the proper points.

However, it's distressing to watch this public concern — letter writing campaigns, contributions of time and money, lobbying, media coverage, etc. — dissipated among subordinate issues and not going where it can do the most good for the grizzly. What's best for the bear must get priority.

Unfortunately, this hasn't been the case. Enthusiasm has gone — and is still going — to subordinate issues. And to most Americans, these emotion-filled secondary disputes are *the grizzly story,* since this is what the media brings them. Although concentrating on less meaningful controversies encourages more public sentiment for the grizzly, it doesn't address the central problems and, in some cases, even worsens the big bear's dilemma.

FEUD AT YELLOWSTONE

Since Congress created Yellowstone National Park in 1872, the park bears — both black and grizzly — have enjoyed a special place in the hearts of millions of Americans. Hoping to see a grizzly, vacationers soon began flocking to the wildlife paradise.

Hotels and campgrounds sprouted like mushrooms on park meadows to accommodate the tourists, and before long, resort operators began to associate big bears with big profits. Garbage pits were therefore strategically situated near hotels to facilitate bear viewing.

When the grizzly, unlike the wolf or mountain lion, started to relate man with food (garbage), the dumps quickly became part of the bear's life. The legendary grizzly, the "great white bear," as the silvertip has been known since the days of Lewis and Clark, became a bum, a wino of the animal world. But the big bears didn't mind. And the tourists loved it, as more and more came to marvel at the mighty grizzly, not caring that he was now a free-loading hobo.

"And you surely ought to see the bears, there are about fifty grizzlies, almost all congregated about the hotels and camps where they find living easy at the garbage piles," urged M.P. Skinner, in his 1926 piece, *The Yellowstone Nature Book.* "At Old Faithful, Lake, Canyon and Mammoth there are established places for them."

"Strangest of all, our bears are peaceable and will not harm you if you let them alone," Skinner boasted. "Where bears are hunted they soon learn the range of modern rifles and how to avoid them; here, the same intelligence tells them they are safe and that it is much easier to eat at the 'bear piles' than to forage for themselves. It has amazed everyone to see how quiet and peaceable the grizzlies have become; because in the days of Lewis and Clark, these big bears were thought to be very ferocious."

Perhaps the excitement and pleasure visitors received from seeing grizzlies allowed the bear to escape the early control measures exerted on the cougar and wolf within the park. Early naturalists and park personnel were unaware, though, that the "quiet and peaceable" grizzly, now a rank scavenger, was destined to clash with man, casting the park into a heated, long-lasting controversy.

By 1916, when the National Park Service (NPS) was formed to take control of the park, a pattern had already been set. The hotels and campgrounds were established fact, and thousands of tourists were eagerly traveling to Yellowstone every summer, all hoping to see a grizzly.

Before 1930, most visitors came by train and stayed in park lodgings. Then dirt roads punched through the Yellowstone wilderness made way for the horseless carriage, further increasing human use of the grizzly's domain, although most visitors still stayed at conveniently located inns.

Later, the modern automobile and better roads opened the wildlife sanctuary to middle-class America. Camping became popular, and the recreational vehicle industry prospered. A mere trickle of tourists became a virtual flood, reaching the million-per-year mark in the early 1950s and bringing difficult, if not unsolvable, sanitation and bear problems.

"In those early days, one of the easiest problems to 'solve' was that of garbage disposal," wrote A.S. Johnson, in the February 1972 issue of the *National Parks and Conservation* magazine. "All that was needed was to dump the garbage in a hole and let the bears, both black and grizzly, eat their fill. In this way most of the garbage was disposed of, the bears obviously liked the arrangement, and the practice was immensely popular with park visitors, who were able to watch the show."

So popular was this free lunch, in fact, that park hotels competed with each other to see who could attract the most bears. More garbage meant more bears, and more bears meant more money. And the bears obliged.

"Soon the Park Service became enmeshed in the business of feeding bears, and it went to extremes in facilitating tourist viewing of the bears," Johnson notes. "Bleacher seats were built; lights were furnished; garbage was even sorted for the bears. One retired park employee recalls the distribution of edible garbage on 'tables,' that visitors might have a better view of the bears as they fed. Another common practice was purposeful placement of items like bacon, which usually provoked a battle between bears."

Before long, people associated bears with Yellowstone. Visitors expected to see bears in the park, just as they expected Old Faithful to perform. Even worse, by his very presence, the grizzly unknowingly helped promote the park's rapidly expanding tourist industry, to the bear's own detriment.

Park administrators finally recognized this collision course between bear and man, but actions to allay the problem arrived slowly. Although official policy in the 1930s asserted, "park objectives to preserve a grizzly population under natural conditions and provide for the safety of visitors," the park still fed bears for public viewing until 1941. Only a shortage of manpower brought on by World War II prompted the closing of several dumps. At this time, Johnson noted, rangers killed 28 grizzlies and 54 black bears as they mobbed the campgrounds looking for the garbage the closed dumps denied them.

Closing a few dumps didn't solve the problem, since bears still fed at several garbage pits which remained open, out of sight, but near campgrounds. Instead of viewing bears at dumps, tourists fed them along roads and in campgrounds.

Yellowstone's panhandling bears caused some of America's first traffic jams. However, these "bear-jams" were mostly the work of black bears. Some grizzlies roamed the campgrounds at night, and an occasional silvertip could be spotted along the highways. But apparently, the grizzly couldn't quite lower his level of intolerance of man to allow the roadside begging. Nonetheless, grizzlies still fed regularly on garbage.

Regardless of the merits of this arrangement, the people enjoyed it. Thus, the Park Service's tardiness in correcting it was predictable.

Soon, tourists became ridiculous in their efforts to see or feed bears. They forgot that these were *wild* animals, and not surprisingly, bear-caused injuries became more common.

In July 1960, the parks distributed its "Bear Management Program and Guidelines," which was the first big step in erasing a long-established American tradition, the beggar bears of Yellowstone.

In a cover letter to the plan, Acting NSP Director Tolson noted: "The uniform and strict application of this program is aimed at a reduction in the number of personal injuries and the amount of property damage caused by bears.... Originally, the bears were self-reliant," Tolson added, "but through inadequate management techniques over a period of years, many have lost these desirable traits. We are now confronted with the problem of re-establishing a wholly wild population...."

Tolson stressed that park visitors were entitled to see bears, but not as they had in the past. "Excessive and unnatural bear populations concentrated along the park roads and in the campgrounds is hardly proper or natural," he said. From then on, visitors were to view wildlife only under normal conditions.

Slowly, but surely, park officials closed the roadside carnival. However, several major dumps remained open, and the bears still gobbled up garbage nearly as fast as man could create it.

In 1959, two wildlife researchers, Drs. Frank and John Craighead, came to Yellowstone. With blessings from all corners, they embarked on a comprehensive study of the Yellowstone grizzlies. At first, it appeared the researchers would provide invaluable advice in helping the National Park Service solve man-bear problems. In the end, however, the exact opposite prevailed.

Armed with adequate funding,[1] modern equipment, and a battery of qualified graduate students, the Craighead brothers began to unravel bear mysteries. For 12 years, they tranquilized, marked, wired, captured, tracked, photographed, measured, and observed some 900 grizzlies. They also started pulling the grizzly's fourth molar and using a cross-section of it to precisely determine the bear's age.[2]

Informed of this research project through popular articles and films, the public hoped it would provide the key to the bear's deliverance. Sadly, results didn't meet the expectations.

A new park superintendent, Jack Anderson, and biologist, Glen Cole, arrived at Yellowstone. Before long, the new officials and the Craigheads began bickering over bear management. In 1971, after years of arguing, the debate deadlocked. The Park Service slammed the door in the Craigheads' face. And the research ended.

Ironically, both Cole and the Craigheads championed the same cause — restoration of a wholly wild grizzly population with an all-natural diet. Exactly how to reach this goal — in other words, how to close the dumps — was the problem.

The Craigheads preferred slowly "phasing out" the garbage pits, gradually easing the bear back into its natural niche. However, the NPS disagreed, Cole suggesting "cold turkey" instead. Park officials quickly used their administrative powers to close the dumps more rapidly than the Craigheads had recommended.

In 1974, the Craigheads publicly declared the Yellowstone grizzly in serious trouble — primarily because of NPS mismanagement. "If the present management continues," Frank Craighead predicted, "it will wipe out the grizzly by about 1990." He said the population had been cut in half in a scant three years — 1970-1972. "We believe there are somewhere in the neighborhood of 100 grizzlies left."

Instead of switching to natural food, the bears had headed for campgrounds, ranches, and tourists camps in search of garbage, according to the Craigheads. Here, bears became "marauders" and were usually

[1]The 12-year Craighead study was funded by the National Geographic Society, Philco Corporation, Bureau of Sport Fisheries and Wildlife (now the U.S. Fish and Wildlife Service), Montana Department of Fish and Game, University of Montana, New York Zoological Society, Boone and Crockett Club, Wildlife Management Institute, National Park Service, Environmental Research Institute, the Atomic Energy Commission, and the National Science Foundation.

[2]Scientists can determine age by counting the layers of enamel on the tooth, one of which is laid down each year.

killed. Officials trapped a few grizzlies and transplanted them into nearby backcountry, but the bears often returned to cause more trouble. These repeated offenders were either sent to zoos or killed.

Writing in *National Wildlife,* Frank Craighead noted, "During 1970-72, there were a total of 118 known grizzly bear deaths in the Yellowstone ecosystem. During our nine years of intensive study, we found that the population increased by about six grizzlies per year. In the five years of new management policies [the NPS policies],the conditions completely changed and mortalities have greatly exceeded births. If this policy continues, it will eliminate the grizzly in this area."

The Craigheads insisted that almost every grizzly in the park area sooner or later visited one of the dumps. With this assumption, they said they could feed their data into a computer and expect valid conclusions. And their computer analysis gave the Yellowstone grizzly only about 30 years to live.

The Park Service violently objected to this method. Citing their data, they reassured the public there were actually two separate grizzly populations in the area — one that visited the dumps regularly and another that never fed on garbage, a wild, free ranging bear population.

Park officials termed the Craighead computer data "completely false." In rebuttal, Glen Cole claimed that data on garbage dump bears was completely different from data on free-ranging, wild grizzlies.

If one puts garbage dump data into the computer, expect to get garbage-dump data out, he asserted. "Just because you use a computer, that doesn't mean it's accurate."

Cole insisted deaths were not exceeding births, and his field observations and Washington boss, Nathaniel Reed, Assistant Interior Secretary for Fish, Wildlife and Parks, backed him up. "Due to the public controversy" Reed declared, "I fielded a special study team which last year [1973] reported no 'crash' in the grizzly population.

"The matter was debated at the time the decision was made," Reed continued, "and the National Park Service Science Advisory Committee firmly and unequivocally supported the decision that the dumps be closed quickly.

"Now that the dumps have been closed, we certainly should address ourselves to the future."

A.S. Johnson, southwest representative of Defenders of Wildlife, detailed both views in his article "Yellowstone Grizzlies: Endangered or Prospering?" After his study, he leaned towards the Park Service position, which at that time was definitely a minority opinion among environmental groups, as most favored the Craighead story.

Using all available sources of information, Johnson wrote, "It was determined by this writer that the present number of grizzlies and the apparent increased breeding success in 1972 and 1973 do not support the prediction of extinction."

"Extinction for the grizzly, or for any form of life, can be predicted only if death rate exceeds its birth rate," he continued. "There is ample data to refute that this condition exists now [October, 1973], and there are strong indications that the condition did not exist even during the high removal rates in 1970 and 1971. Current high reproductive success in the Yellowstone grizzly would certainly appear to deny any prediction of future extinction."

All this brawling only confused a concerned public, which was waiting for someone to agree on the best plan to help the grizzly. Most citizen groups interpreted the park view as bad news for the grizzly. After all, there were many examples of bureaucratic bungling to cite. It might be different this time, but they weren't prepared to take the chance. Sooner or later, most conservationists sided with the Craigheads, actively castigating the Park Service.

"We believe that the conclusions of the Craigheads are based on a far more extensive and methodologically sound program of research, which has yielded a greater volume of much broader data," Tom Garrett, wildlife director for Friends of the Earth noted in a view common to conservation groups. "We expect, therefore, that the Craigheads' appreciation of the present status of the grizzly population is far more likely to be correct than that prepared by Mr. Cole of the National Park Service."

From here the situation worsened to the present bitter impasse. The last link was broken in 1972, when a research agreement, which required the Craigheads to rely on spoonfed information from the NPS and prohibited any public contact without a clearance from Washington, went unsigned. Claiming this agreement made a "farce of scientific research and muzzled academic freedom," the Craigheads refused to sign, thus completely breaking what at best had been a tenuous relationship. The brothers packed up their tranquilizer guns and left the park.

About this time, the press gave the controversy high priority, and many flashy articles and commentaries followed. Park officials were labeling the Craigheads as cranks. On the other hand, many conservationalists viewed the park personnel as bloodthirsty bear exterminators. (Some stories even falsely implied that the park *wanted* to wipe out the grizzly to solve a long-standing headache.)

Never before in the history of wildlife management has there been a complete breakdown in communication between scientific researchers. The Craigheads gave total blame to the Park Service and its parent bureaucracy, the U.S. Department of the Interior. "When the present superintendent [Jack Anderson], and National Park Service biologist [Glen Cole] moved into Yellowstone, they probably felt our research was a threat, because from research you get information and conclusions that may be contrary to existing policy," Frank Craighead challenged. "Many bureaucratic administrators fear research findings that indicate a need for policy changes, especially from sources they can't control."

During their last years in the park, the Craigheads complained of NPS harassment. The Yellowstone Park Company, a commercial enterprise operating park concessions, had provided the Craigheads with a building for housing and storage, but the NPS burned it down. Research efforts were, in general, undermined — including removal of tags from study bears without notifying the Craigheads. The reserachers were even denied information in park rangers' logs.

"No attempt was made to coordinate their [NPS] research with ours," Frank Craighead accused. "The park failed to honor our research contracts; professional ethics were violated."

He summarized the park's action as a "systematic, deliberate, destruction of a research project that would have greatly benefited the park.

"The record is very clear. Because our findings were contrary to existing policy, the results of our research activities in the park and our research techniques have been thoroughly misrepresented by certain members of the Park Service. Not only the researcher, but his conclusions too must conform to bureaucratic mandate.

"A Park Service superintendent, and especially at Yellowstone, has near dictatorial powers," Frank Craighead charged.

Predictably, the Park Service blamed the Craigheads. "Some people just have to have their way," Cole remarked, obviously referring to the Craigheads and implying immature attitudes. "They wanted garbage fed for 10 more years, and we wouldn't have it. So they went to the press."

Cole doesn't like the way the media handled the debate, commenting, "Stop agonizing over the past. There's nothing to gain by biologists tearing people apart in the press. I truly believe we hurt the grizzly by this."

Apparently, relations between park officials and the Craigheads had gone well at Yellowstone until Anderson and Cole moved into the park in 1967.

44

Anderson wanted a clean sweep for the park's 100th birthday (1972). Remembering his first days at the park, he recalls, "There were certain things I very firmly didn't like." Apparently, one of these was the Craighead research project.

Noting that he forbade his own rangers to visit the garbage dumps, Anderson complained about the Craigheads bringing in journalists, personal guests, and even their own children. The superintendent also objected to the radio transmitters and vividly colored streamers the researchers attached to bears because all this paraphernalia seemed out of place on what were supposed to be wild animals.

Furthermore, he worried about campers confronting a grizzly that had just been tranquilized, saddled with electronic gadgetry, and a fluorescent orange necktie, and worked over by an amateur dentist.

Finally, he said the brothers occupied a rent-free old and unsightly building the park wanted to remove before the centennial. Countering the Craigheads' charge of lack of information, Anderson said the researchers likewise declined to release any of their data to park officials.

To Anderson, the issue boiled down to whether outside professors could "go romping around the woods," pulling grizzly teeth and decorating bears, leaving him to take the consequences.

"It's a shame," John Craighead admitted, "because I'm sure the Park Service is as interested in saving the grizzly bear as we are. It has got into these social and political issues that are bigger problems than the bears themselves."

The scientific fraternity didn't like the squabble either. "The National Park Service is responsible for the controversy which should never have occurred," charged Laurence M. Gould, former president of the American Association for the Advancement of Science.

"In 1963," he continued, "the National Academy of Sciences recommended that the Park Service should make every effort to support and accommodate independent research and should recognize that basic research of this kind will enhance the importance of the national parks and will contribute to the interpretational functions of the service and to our national scientific effort."

"When the Craigheads began their work with the grizzlies in Yellowstone Park in 1959, they received the friendliest kind of cooperation and encouragement from the then-Supt. Lemuel Garrison," Gould recalled. When the present Supt. Jack Anderson took charge in 1968, that policy was "abruptly terminated," followed by a period of harassment.

"To have continued to work in Yellowstone Park, the Craigheads would have been required to submit to such restrictions as no self-respecting scientist could accept and which would have made their research impossible," Gould continued. "They had no choice but to withdraw.

"There is no point in trying to understand the grizzly population unless a quantitative study of their numbers can be made. No one has devised a more reliable method than that followed by the Craigheads. To pretend that this is a hardship on the bears is sentimental nonsense."

Criticism kept coming, most of it directed at the Park Service. Therefore, in an attempt to clear up the situation once and for all, Interior Secretary Rogers C.B. Morton again asked the National Academy of Sciences to sort out facts from fiction and make recommendations on the management of Yellowstone grizzlies. Upon hearing this, both feuding parties publicly declared they were confident that prestigious scientists would confirm their convictions, and after the report emerged in June, 1974, both parties publicly declared it confirmed their convictions.

The NPS rushed out a news release saying the report verified their management policies. They quoted a key conclusion of the report: "There is no convincing evidence that the grizzly bears in the Yellowstone ecosystem are in immediate danger of extinction." Anyone reading this statement would assume the park had been right all along.

However, the Park Service press releases ignored the following points: The study had chastised the park for not having sufficient data on which to base a management plan, had generally supported the Craighead research, and had recommended prompt funding of a comprehensive research study by qualified independent scientists.

In fact, the first recommendation of the 1974 report read, "We recommend that the National Park Service and the U.S. Forest Service pursue a policy of supporting and encouraging independent research of Yellowstone grizzlies. The freedom of scientists to conduct research through the Yellowstone ecosystem is imperative if the data essential to successfully manage Yellowstone grizzlies is to be obtained: the presence of independent investigators will enhance and invigorate study programs undertaken by land management agencies."

Later on, the study team noted, "The research program carried out by the National Park Service administration since 1970 has been inadequate to provide the data essential for devising sound management policies for the grizzly bears in the Yellowstone ecosystem."

When asked by the *Jackson Hole News* why park biologists had no data on grizzly populations for the past three years (1971-74), Anderson replied, "We have been concentrating more on people management rather than bear management." He also said it was his task to protect both bears and people.

He further stated that the park had developed better census techniques than the Craigheads had — namely, aerial photography and sightings by trained individuals.

"We're finding grizzly," Anderson reassured. "My concern would be that because of the low subadult mortality, the numbers might be getting too high."

Angered over this reaction, Professor Gould declared, "The National Park Service appears to wish to downgrade and discredit the academy report for which it asked and for which it paid. Coupled with its continuing effort to downgrade the research of the Craighead brothers and their colleagues, this constitutes a gross affront to the scientific community.

"No national park should be managed as the feudal domain of the superintendent," Gould continued, "The national parks belong to all of us, especially Yellowstone, which is surely one of the finest outdoor research laboratories in the world. This is the second time in a few years that the National Park Service has requested the advice and recommendations of the National Academy of Sciences. For the second time, it would turn aside from the recommendations as if it were above criticism.

"It is high time that the academic community expressed its vigorous opposition to such authoritarian policies which are totally foreign to the spirit of science," Gould concluded.

Who was right — park officials or the Craigheads? Regrettably, under the present situation, concerned citizens can only answer this frequently asked question by waiting. If the bear population plummets to the verge of extinction, the Craigheads were right. And the grizzly has lost.

Park biologists may have been right. The population may be leveling out at the correct level after a few declining years. Even so, should they have taken the chance — especially when their scientific information was scanty compared to the Craigheads' massive collection of research data? This decision could have meant disaster for the Yellowstone grizzly. Would it have been better to accept the Craigheads' recommendations — just in case? Then, any error would have at least been on the side of the grizzly.

Regardless, it now seems appropriate to put the Yellowstone feud on the back burner. *Who* was right seems less serious than *what* is right for the grizzly now and in the future.

THE ULTIMATE TROPHY

The grizzly's reputation — fierce, awesome, and dangerous — quickly made him one of the most prized game animals. Many early bear hunters came home with colorful tales of charging grizzlies that had absorbed slug after slug with little apparent effect. Often, the story tellers ended their campfire yarn with the grizzly finally falling dead at the hunter's feet, a split-second "before he ripped me apart."

Theodore Roosevelt, America's most famous big game hunter, shot several silvertips. He labeled the grizzly "the king of game beasts in temperate North America." Enos A. Mills, in his book *The Grizzly, Our Greatest Wild Animal,* noted, "...In the hunting industry, the grizzly heads the list. The hunter will pay more for a shot at a grizzly than for a shot at any other, and often all other game. Hunters frequently spend from one thousand to many thousands of dollars going after the grizzly. They will work harder and longer for a grizzly than for any other animal." He made this astute observation in 1919.

Later, other early hunters and outdoor writers further glamorized the grizzly as the superior trophy. The stigma stuck, for today, a grizzly conquered in a fair, man-against-beast contest in a harsh environment is still considered the ultimate trophy by many sportsmen.

However, times are changing. Although a small circle of hunters still see the silvertip as the summit of their sport, many more people abhor grizzly hunting. In fact, national sentiment may be turning away from all hunting as an accepted pastime. Much to the dismay of America's 16 million hunters, millions of nonhunters — mostly urbanites — want to stop all shooting of wildlife, and grizzly hunting is especially infuriating to hunter-haters.

With the great Yellowstone debate still making headlines and creating a general doomsday image for all grizzlies, no-hunt forces figured the time was right to expand their efforts to save the silvertip. They turned on the sportsman, but unfortunately, they again missed the mark as they unwittingly exaggerated a second subordinate issue.

On November 15, 1973, Friends of the Earth, the Sierra Club, and the National Parks and Conservation Association asked the U.S. Forest Service (FS) to ban grizzly hunting in national forests in the Yellowstone Park area. (In reality, such a ban would totally terminate grizzly hunting around the park. Outside the park, the big bear's range almost exclusively is on national forest land.)

"In our opinion," the three citizens' groups wrote to FS Chief John

McGuire, "it behooves the management agency on whose lands the grizzly bear is being unnecessarily killed to take the conservative position — and thereby assure the survival of the bear. In this case, the easiest and quickest way to reduce mortality of the grizzly bears in the Yellowstone ecosystem is to temporarily close the hunting season in the relevant parts of Wyoming and Montana."

The three organizations insisted the FS had the authority to close the season. As a case in point, they reminded McGuire that in 1970 Minnesota's Superior National Forest banned the killing of the eastern timber wolf. "Minor differences between this case and that one are not relevant when the extinction of a species over an area as large as the Yellowstone ecosystem is predicted by competent scientists."

To this request, the FS gave a polite "no."[1] "The States [Montana and Wyoming] do not feel that the number of bears taken in the national forests under [state game] regulations is a threat to the continued existence of a viable, healthy population of grizzly bears," McGuire explained.

The FS chief also felt the difference between the wolf and grizzly situations was significant. "In the first place, the Eastern timber wolf was — and is — on the endangered species list," he wrote. "Secondly, Minnesota state laws did not, and still do not, afford any protection to the Eastern timber wolf. Finally, the action in Minnesota was taken in the face of an impending massive trapping effort which could have had a major impact on the local wolf population."

Although stymied in this first round, anti-hunters kept pressure on the FS. In August 1974, the same three groups joined with seven more[2] and again demanded that the FS close to grizzly hunting the national forest land around Yellowstone Park.

Apparently, McGuire was more shaken by this additional public concern than he had been by the first request. Shortly thereafter (September 12,

[1]Mostly because of cooperative agreements that emphasize the state's right to manage nonmigratory wildlife, the FS refused to ban hunting. However, the federal agency does indeed have the statutory authority to do so. Russell P. McRorey, Acting Deputy Chief of the FS, explains, "The Forest Service has authority and could legally control use and occupancy of National Forest System lands for the purpose of protecting the grizzly bear and its habitat. In essence, this represents a ban on hunting by prohibiting use of National Forest System lands for taking of the grizzly bear."

[2]Audubon Society, Humane Society of the United States, Defenders of Wildlife, Animal Protection Institute, Environmental Defense Fund, New York Zoological Society, and The Wilderness Society.

1974), he asked Montana to close the hunting districts around the park. (Wyoming had already temporarily closed the season.)

"After careful consideration of all the information I have been able to obtain," McGuire wrote to Wes Woodgerd, director of the Montana Department of Fish and Game, "I have concluded that the action these organizations have asked me to take is neither necessary nor desirable. Furthermore, it would be counter to the longstanding cooperative agreement under which the Forest Service and the Montana Department of Fish and Game manage wildlife and wildlife habitat inside the National Forests.

"I believe these organizations, as well as other organizations and individuals who are pressuring both you and me for additional closures, are sincere. Therefore, to help allay their fears, I hope you will give consideration to closure of additional areas of the Gallatin National Forest that are considered by some people to be a part of the Yellowstone ecosystem. I make this suggestion even though you folks believe, and we concur, that this will not have much influence on actual hunting take of grizzly bears."

Following this request, the Montana Fish and Game Commission did indeed stop all hunting around Yellowstone Park, as the citizen groups had demanded.

Even with this "victory," however, anti-hunters didn't relax. Next, their attention turned to the citizens' participation section of the newly passed Endangered Species Act of 1973.

Fund for Animals, Inc.,[1] a well-known eastern preservationist group, surged to the front line to save the grizzly. Citing the Endangered Species Act, on February 14, 1974, the Fund petitioned the U.S. Department of the Interior to make the grizzly an endangered species.

"We believe there is neither scientific nor legal justification for another hunter to take one more grizzly bear within the lower 48 states," was the Fund's blunt conclusion.

Along with the petition, the Fund submitted 17 exhibits which, according to petitioners Lewis Regenstein and Stephen R. Seater, "...demonstrate a severely reduced and rapidly dwindling grizzly bear population in recent

---

[1]The Fund for Animals, Inc. is a well-organized and influential preservationist group specifically interested in stopping hunting and trapping. Based in New York, the organization has seven regional offices spread out across the nation and some "well-knowns" on their national board — Doris Day, Dick Cavett, Steve Allen, Angie Dickinson, Rod McKuen, Jayne Meadows, Susan Saint James, Dick Van Dyke, and Gretchen Wyler. As of February 1, 1975, Cleveland Amory, President, claimed 100,000 members.

50

years, federal and state management policies exacerbating this trend, and predictions by the foremost grizzly bear experts in the world that, absent a speedy reversal of these policies, the grizzly bear in the Yellowstone ecosystem will be extinct by the year 2000 or possibly sooner."

In general, all 17 exhibits came directly or indirectly from the Craigheads. Many were Craighead scientific publications. But a few letters from various officials citing a scarcity of good data were included.

Interestingly, almost all the supporting exhibits referred only to the Yellowstone situation, not to northwestern Montana, which has a larger expanse of occupied grizzly habitat and probably more bears, than the Yellowstone Park area. Nonetheless, the petitioners wanted the bear classed as endangered and hunting banned "in the lower 48 states," not merely in the Yellowstone Park area.

State officials claimed the grizzly population in northwestern Montana was stable or even increasing. But the Fund wouldn't accept this. It called the game department's information scanty and insisted Interior should "be conservative" when the fate of an entire species was at stake. To compensate for lack of data from other grizzly ranges, the Fund said there was no reliable information refuting their allegations that the bear is endangered.

When first introduced, the petition caused an uproar. Then, most observers forgot it, thinking it would be buried like most pleas sent to the Washington bureaucracy. Several months later, however, the Interior Department — through the U.S. Fish and Wildlife Service's Endangered Species Office — began distributing "Position Paper — Grizzly Bear."

Interior Department heavyweights had been pressured to make the grizzly an endangered species. On the other hand, game departments, a few wildlife scientists, and some sportsmen wanted bear management left to the states without classifying the grizzly under the Endangered Species Act.

In typical bureaucratic and political fashion, Interior had conjured up a compromise to please everybody, but managed to please only a few, if any, Americans closely watching the agency's actions. Instead of siding with either side, Interior recommended "threatened" status which meant the situation was less serious than "endangered."[1] The Interior Department — again acting through the U.S. Fish and Wildlife Service (FWS) — also

---

[1]The Endangered Species Act of 1973 defines "endangered" species as "any species which is in danger of extinction throughout all or a significant portion of its range...." The Act defines a "threatened" species as "...any species which is likely to become an endangered species within the foreseeable future throughout all or a significant portion of its range."

51

divided grizzly range into three "ecosystems" — Yellowstone, Bob Marshall, and Selway/Bitterroot, and allowed sportsmen to hunt a few grizzlies in the Bob Marshall.

In response, the International Association of Game, Fish and Conservation Commissioners[1] (a group composed of state wildlife agency commissioners) attacked the FWS decision: "We submit that the Director [of the FWS] has failed to take account of available scientific evidence. We see no evidence that the Secretary [of Interior] has taken into consideration the efforts of Idaho, Montana and Wyoming to conserve grizzly bears...." To back up his organization's charges, Executive Vice President John Gottschalk, quoted the National Academy of Sciences report: "There is no convincing evidence that the grizzly bears in the Yellowstone Ecosystem are in immediate danger of extinction."

"The proposal to list the grizzly bear as a threatened species is not supported by the best available scientific evidence as required by the Endangered Species Act," Gottschalk concluded. "Indeed, the best available scientific evidence suggests that grizzly populations, except possibly in the Yellowstone area, are generally stable."

Also objecting to the FWS position, Lewis Regenstein, Executive Vice President of Fund for Animals, publicly declared that Interior had "caved in to the trophy hunting lobby. Here you have the Interior Department formally endorsing large-scale hunting of an animal they admit is a threatened species — it's mockery."

The position paper began boldly: "The United States Fish and Wildlife Service takes the position that the grizzly bear is threatened in the United States south of Canada." Then, it went on to explain the statement — inadequately, according to most observers.

Although the authors mentioned that the impact of increased bear-man conflict produced by recreational development and new roads into grizzly habitat was the main reason for the species' precarious position, they developed this idea no further. After this token statement, the paper addressed the hunting controversy. The authors included recommendations for "taking" grizzlies, but not a single word about curbing continued inroads into grizzly habitat on federal land or about limiting recreational and residential development.

[1]This organization later changed its name to International Association of Fish and Wildlife Agencies.

Also, the paper pointed out a severe conflict with livestock grazing on publicly owned grizzly habitat. But instead of suggesting cutting back on grazing allotments, the authors mentioned the possibility of compensating ranchers for predation — a cosmetic treatment that ignores the basic problem.

Basically, the hunting argument centered on the idea that there was insufficient data to prove hunting wasn't endangering the species. Preservation groups wanted federal authorities to take the safe "conservative position" and stop hunting. "Better safe, than sorry," they argued.

On the contrary, wildlife managers insisted that ample information was available, although they admitted it could be more conclusive. But even if the necessary data wasn't at hand, the states countered, the Fish and Wildlife Service must wait until evidence became available (as required by the Endangered Species Act) before classifying the bear. Or if the agency had to act now, it should follow the Act's guidelines and use the best available information, which, according to the game departments, indicated the bear population was secure.

Obviously, Interior leaned toward the conservative position, even though they knew it would mean sharp criticism from the states.

Specifically, the arguments against and for grizzly hunting line up as follows:

TO BAN GRIZZLY HUNTING

1. Although grizzly bear mortality occurs in many ways, hunting is the easiest and quickest to curb. Harry B. Crandell, former director of Wilderness Reviews for The Wilderness Society, summed up this position in a September 17, 1974, letter to Wes Woodgerd. "Habitat protection is basic to wildlife management, but we wish to again state our view that the total man-caused loss of grizzly bear is more than the species can stand at this time, based on the report of the National Academy of Sciences, which sets this figure at 'about ten.'

"Keeping this limitation in mind, we note the following from Kenneth Greer's [Montana Department of Fish and Game employee] report on Montana Grizzly Bear Management: 'Apparently, several grizzly bear populations occur in Montana, providing an annual hunting harvest if kept at acceptable levels. Other forms of annual mortality which occur are more difficult to manage.' It seems to us this is the crux of the problem. You have the power to apply the surest and perhaps easiest means of helping the grizzlies over the present emergency.

"Not too much can be done right now, as we understand it, about killings resulting from poaching, stock depredations and public safety considerations. We realize that lawful sport hunters would bear the burden of temporary control measures of this kind but we believe they are likely to be more understanding than most. Your department right now is the best friend the grizzly bear has in his battle for survival in Montana.

"We can all work toward preserving habitat but if hunting mortality continues to exceed total permissible population reductions, the problem will have worsened substantially by the time protective action really takes place. The problem may have the classic signs of too little, too late, so familiar to all of us who have spent our lives in wildlife management.

2. A hunting ban would immediately eliminate "enough" mortality to make up for low reproductive success in the Yellowstone Park area. The Craigheads publicly declared that National Park Service mismanagement of the Yellowstone population had caused the death rate to vastly exceed the birth rate — a death wish for any species. They claimed the grizzly would disappear from the Yellowstone area "about 1990" and a drastic step — i.e. an immediate ban on hunting — was needed to help level out the death/birth ratio. After the situation stabilized, perhaps hunting could be reintroduced as part of the management plan in some areas, but a moratorium was needed in face of this emergency.

3. The "accessibility" of local grizzly populations hasn't received enough consideration. Although grizzlies in remote habitat might sustain their numbers during hunting pressure, a highly accessible population would not. Since hunters naturally concentrate in areas with the easiest access, the quota for a large area can be filled or almost filled from a few drainages with good access.

This was a major point made by Douglas H. Chadwick in the study of grizzlies in the Swan Range in northwestern Montana. Chadwick believes that most drainages around the Bob Marshall Wilderness now have, or soon will have, road access, and that added accessibility will allow hunters to put unexpected stress on local bear populations, even to the extent of eliminating bears from certain drainages. Even though the harvest remains reasonably stable, Chadwick notes, too much of the quota could be coming from small accessible areas which are overhunted.

Andy Russell, author of *Grizzly Country* agrees with Chadwick. "Access roads, in conjunction with harvest-type management, have also allowed for overkill by hunters," he notes. "When large numbers of hunters can reach into almost every valley, they are a threat to the big bear. Even if they do not shoot him, the noise and continued disturbance often causes him to move to another area far less favorably disposed to hold him. This is what is meant by habitat destruction."

4. Population level unknown. Since state wildlife managers can't give critics an accurate estimate of the number of grizzlies, many citizens conclude hunting should cease until a close census is completed.

5. Hunting may technically violate the Endangered Species Act. Russell W. Peterson, Chairman of the President's Council on Environmental Quality, strongly suggested this in an April 22, 1975 letter to Rogers Morton, then Secretary of the Interior.

6. Since grizzly numbers have been thinned from several hundred thousand to a few hundred, the species must be endangered and may soon be extinct.

7. Montana allows an unlimited number of hunters. Sometimes the number of permits exceeds the estimate of the total grizzly population so a single season could wipe out the species. Washington Post columnist Jack Anderson, emphasized this point in one of his nationally circulated columns. "Conservationists estimate that only about 900 of these magnificent carnivores still survive in the lower 48 states," Anderson wrote. "Yet, the state of Montana, where the largest population of grizzlies exists, issued 919 grizzly permits for this year's [1974] hunting season. If only a small number of these hunters are successful, the entire species could be nearly wiped out in the area."

8. Since the sport is inadequately regulated, illegal kills are common. No evidence exists that authorities can curb poaching in the future. The scarcity of enforcement personnel and the vastness of grizzly country hamper anti-poaching efforts.

9. We're taking an unlimited harvest from a limited resource. This is the strong point Dr. John Craighead made in his February 25, 1972, letter to Willis B. Jones, former Chairman of the Montana Fish and Game Commission. "...I think it is important for the Commission to recognize that we are now taking an unlimited harvest against an unknown resource. This is a gamble and, moreover, it is a gamble in a high risk situation. Stated in the simplest terms, the Commission has nothing to lose by underharvest but everything to lose by overharvest."

Craighead further confirmed his view in a personal discussion. Although he condones grizzly hunting, he fears the data to justify it right now isn't available. "Mortality should be kept as low as possible until there is absolute

55

evidence that the population is holding its own or increasing," he declared. "The way things are set up now, we won't know *in time* if hunting is having an impact. A steady harvest is not an absolute indicator that the population is not in trouble."

10. Sound data is lacking. Even if Interior doesn't completely agree with Craighead's warning, the department lacks the facts to refute it and therefore must put an immediate ban on grizzly hunting. "We are in no position to defend either the Montana Cooperative Wildlife Research Unit [the Craigheads] or the National Park Service, with regard to the status of the grizzly bear population in the Yellowstone Ecosystem," the position paper authors admitted. "Nevertheless, with the survival or extinction of a native species at stake, we feel it is advisable not to ignore the more pessimistic view of the Montana Cooperative Wildlife Research Unit." The federal agency said it would have no qualms about hunting if there were conclusive proof that the bear population could sustain it.

11. Since the Forest Service has refused to stop hunting on national forest lands, listing the grizzly under the Endangered Species Act represents the silvertip's last hope.

12. Nationally, people don't want grizzly hunting. This point — the social objection — is undoubtedly the most difficult to address. Biological justification for some grizzly hunting may be available or forthcoming, but even with it, some people would rather see the bear "harvested" *in any manner* other than hunting.

In a limited habitat, a population of any species (grizzly included) will produce a surplus that must be removed somehow. In the grizzly's case, man or other bears are the only predators. So some silvertips will be killed legally or illegally by sportsmen or administrators, as bears move into inhabited areas.

However, preservationists want the balance maintained by means other than hunting. Grizzlies reside almost exclusively on public land, and many people don't want hunting on *their* land.

13. Hunting hinders outmigration. As mentioned in Chapter 6, many conservationists hope to re-establish grizzly populations in wild lands now without the big bears. However, they feel hunting crops surplus bears, thus not allowing population stress to push them into unoccupied habitat. Since a major transplant requires extensive research and time, bear supporters prefer a hunting ban, which may accomplish the re-establishment naturally.

Large grizzly bears such as this one bagged in 1977 by Jack Atcheson, Jr. of Butte, Montana are considered by many sportsmen as the ultimate trophy. Western game departments and some sportsmen support grizzly hunting as part of professional wildlife management. But critics claim hunting is inconsistent with efforts to preserve the threatened grizzly. Who's right?

TO ALLOW GRIZZLY HUNTING

1. Bear numbers will, with regulated sport hunting, remain stable, if the amount and quality of habitat isn't reduced. If habitat encroachment continues unabated, the grizzly population will dwindle with or without hunting. James White, former director of the Wyoming Game and Fish Department, emphasized this point while objecting to the federal government's classification of the grizzly under the Endangered Species Act. "If we closed the season, but still continued to build roads and allowed certain other human activities in the wilderness areas, the grizzly would be gone anyway," White warned.

Montana's official position statement on grizzly management agrees with White's view. "Anti-hunters could better serve the grizzly by relaxing their attacks on sportsmen and joining the move to preserve grizzly habitat."

And Idaho's experience supports the opinions of Montana and Wyoming wildlife managers. Although Idaho closed the season on grizzlies in 1946, the state's grizzly population has continually declined to today's all-time low.

2. Hunting is carefully regulated. Montana and Wyoming have adequate control of the situation with detailed regulations and management plans. "To quickly summarize," Montana's official statement concludes, "we strongly feel legal hunting is *not* endangering the grizzly, and if there was ever the slightest indication that it was, this department would be the first to propose closing the season."

3. In Montana's case, the policy of selling an unlimited number of permits doesn't mean an unlimited harvest. State game managers have watched the situation closely for over 20 years. The success ratio has remained at about 2%, averaging 31.5 bears per year. Joe Egan, assistant administrator of game management for the Montana Department of Fish and Game, feels these figures indicate a stable population. He believes that if these bears weren't taken by hunters, they would be killed by some other means — most likely as "marauders" as they are forced from the remote habitat by population stress.

Grizzly bears are like any other species, Egan notes; there is only so much room for so many individuals, and any surplus will be removed. He says the present license system does an excellent job of removing these extra bears.

Montana also dislikes the permit system Wyoming has used. It is, according to the Environmental Impact Statement on grizzly hunting, prepared by the Department of Fish and Game, "in effect, limiting the number of grizzly bear hunters, rather than the number of bears killed. This would defeat the goal of having sufficient hunters in the field to make bears wary, and probably would not achieve an adequate kill of surplus bears (because hunting success is low). A quota on the number of bears killed is much more direct and manageable. A permit system would also limit the number of sportsmen able to participate in the hunt, depriving them of benefits that accrue even to unsuccessful hunters."

Montana and the federal government worked out a compromise for the 1975 season. Briefly, this agreement allowed only 25 bears to be removed from northwestern Montana, including bears killed for public safety for destroying private property or livestock, illegally, or on Indian reservations. "In a select situation," the game department noted, "The season could close before it opens — if nonhunter deaths tally 25. However, using mortality information from the last few years, we predict that from five to ten grizzlies will be available to hunters. When the total take approaches 25, the season will be closed on a 48-hour notice." In 1975, the first year with the 25 bear quota, hunters harvested 13 grizzlies from northwestern Montana, and 9 more were killed for other reasons before the Department of Fish and Game closed the season. The game department was likewise careful not to exceed the 25-bear limit in 1976, closing the season after 23 grizzlies were killed — 11 by hunters.

4. Foremost bear experts agree grizzlies can be hunted in carefully controlled situations. Dr. John Craighead had this to say in an April 18, 1974, letter to James White, former director of the Wyoming Game and Fish Department. "I personally favor hunting grizzly bears wherever a viable population exists and where, at the same time, action is taken to reduce deaths from poaching and control. A hunter harvest can be closely regulated and supervised and is preferable to control and illegal kills. Research has shown that the latter may increase when hunting is prohibited."

Dr. Charles Jonkel, another bear researcher with unchallengeable credentials, also favors hunting. "Hunting can also be used as a tool to keep animal numbers in balance with habitat components. In this case, by removing surplus bears annually, the hunter precludes the movement of subadult animals into populated areas where they may injure people, kill livestock, and create 'bad press' for the species. In fact, full protection of the grizzly in Yellowstone Park, combined with the National Park Service's 'open-pit' garbage disposal program, led to one of the most tragic examples of wildlife mismanagement in recent years. Merely protecting bears from hunters, therefore, is no solution to bear preservation....Carefully controlled hunting could provide an economical bear management alternative, a culturally rewarding form of recreation, and a reduction in undesirable conflicts between people and bears."

5. The states have a right to manage nonmigratory wildlife. State game departments strongly feel they control resident wildlife even if it's on federal lands, a position supported by legal decisions. Thus, restricting management by classifying the grizzly under the Endangered Species Act is, state game managers believe, a violation of this right. "We have resisted this proposed federal take-over of state jurisdiction and management of resident wildlife species," Woodgerd remarks, "and shall continue to insist that the grizzly will fare better under state control."

6. What regulation will come next? State wildlife managers are reluctant to give ground on grizzly management because of the precedent it would set. They think that other game animals — bighorn sheep, mountain lion, sandhill crane, whistling swan, etc.— will also be classified under the Endangered Species Act and that state regulation will be usurped.

7. Alaska's experiences. Alaska has an increasing number of hunters and an increasing number of grizzlies. Jim Rearden, of the Alaska Board of Game, notes that the average annual kill for the entire state has gone from 595 in 1961-65, to 687 in 1966-70, to 815 in 1971-75. Meanwhile, the bear population is the highest it has been in years and is, in fact, still increasing in some areas.

"The bear population is much higher than it would be if bears were not hunted," Rearden explains. Hunting has stimulated the Alaskan peninsula bear population by altering the sex ratio in favor of young females. Hunters prefer trophies which are often older males. Also, regulations prohibit shooting females with cubs, thus further increasing the percentage of females in the population and, in turn, increasing reproduction. In addition, fewer bears die of old age, as hunters remove the trophy grizzlies.

8. Chadwick's report is misleading. Douglas Chadwick's report, on which no-hunt organizations based much of their case, has been discredited by some wildlife professionals. Briefly, Chadwick concluded that grizzlies disappeared from one drainage after the Forest Service opened it to logging. He said hunters overshot the local grizzly population because of the easy access the logging roads provided.

Some professional observers (Chadwick included) believe this data was blown out of proportion "for political reasons," because it conveniently paralleled the intended conclusion to ban hunting. After the controversy over classifying the grizzly as a threatened species subsided slightly, authorities such as Dr. Charles Jonkel and Dr. W. Leslie Pengelly, who teaches wildlife biology at the University of Montana and was Chadwick's adviser during his study, have criticized the study. Jonkel believes the study "should have been made before, during, and after the logging, not just during." Pengelly notes that Chadwick was studying mountain goats and only made these incidental grizzly observations.

Jonkel, presently conducting a study in the same area, says the drainage has grizzlies now. Furthermore, he has evidence that the drainage may have had grizzlies at the same time Chadwick theorized the population had been wiped out.

9. We already have as many grizzly bears as the available habitat will support. Commenting on the grizzly's threatened status, Woodgerd remarks, "Montana has not only reported a stable (increasing in some areas) grizzly population, but has data to back it up. In fact, I and many other persons, consider the Montana grizzly 'abundant' in several areas, 'common' in other areas and 'infrequent' in some intermediate or traveling areas adjacent to or between habitat."

Grizzlies need lots of room and their numbers can't increase indefinitely in a limited space, according to many state game managers, and remaining grizzly areas have as many bears as this habitat has ever supported.

10. Hunting can actually be beneficial to grizzly populations. Undoubtedly, this is a big pill for bear-lovers to swallow. Nonetheless, noted experts feel this way.

John Craighead, for example, believes "Overpopulation can be easily and quickly rectified by increasing the hunter harvest. A moratorium against killing grizzlies would probably arouse the livestock interests and perhaps others to seek more liberal regulations. It would increase illegal kills and perhaps bear-man conflicts. I do not believe this management alternative is in the interest of the bear, the hunter, the livestock industry, or the general public."

And Jonkel agrees. "Hunting has a beneficial effect on the preservation of the species which can, because of their size and strength, be harmful to people. For instance, hunted grizzlies begin to be wary, to avoid man and areas frequented by him." *If they have any where else to go, that is.*

11. The decision to hunt grizzlies shouldn't depend on political or social pressure. Even a casual student can see that there is some *biological* justification for hunting grizzlies on a limited basis in some areas. However, there may not be *social* justification. Apparently, social objections sometimes take priority over biological facts. Much to the displeasure of professional wildlife biologists, political pressure often dictates biological decisions. "This whole grizzly mess is" according to one of these wildlife biologists, "merely an exercise in bio-politics." (Witness McGuire's request that Montana close the hunting season.)

Sportsmen don't like the idea of management policies decided on nonbiological grounds. But they can't do much about it — except, perhaps, to write editorials, as Terry Sheely did in *Fishing and Hunting News,* a Pacific Northwest tabloid.

In the May 18, 1974, edition, Sheely wrote, in part, "It's tough enough holding back the pack of preservationists maneuvering for a throathold on sport hunting, without being pushed from behind by the guy you thought was watching the back door.

"And lately it feels like we've been hit between the shoulder blades so hard we've got whiplash, not to mention losing another chunk of ground to anti-hunters.

"The most recent incident was the cancellation of scheduled Montana grizzly bear hunts in districts 313, 316, and 371.

"...When preservationists flex their legal muscle, Montana Fish and Game Commissioners suddenly find themselves with a request to cancel the previously scheduled grizzly seasons in districts just outside Yellowstone Park. Now, the commissioners have previously been told by their own grizzly specialists that the Montana grizzly bear population is as sound as a pre-zinc silver dollar, and regulated hunting won't affect the bears one way or another.

"We'd like to say the commissioners told the federal boys, 'Our game managers have proven that grizzlies are not endangered in Montana and that a season is fully justified and will be carried out as such.

"Unfortunately, they didn't say that or anything even like that. They cancelled the seasons. That will probably take a little heat off the thin-skinned boys in Washington and will please the Fund for Animals to no end. After all, they got the season closed and saved the expense of a court fight. That savings alone will leave them with enough money to grubstake another battle against sport hunting," Shelly concluded.

The pro/con discussion was objectively presented, listing every argument, so readers could make up their minds on the deep-rooted question of should there be grizzly hunting. After such an extensive study of both sides of this controversial and complex question, anybody will have opinions, as, understandably, the author does. Of course, readers will probably have different views, but for the record, the author believes:

1. State wildlife agencies have overseeing boards or commissioners who are usually political appointees. From their view, social or political objections take a high place in their thinking — and especially when the heat is on. For this reason, grizzly hunting south of Canada will probably soon become history — regardless of the biological facts involved. *good* ,

2. After sorting out all the arguments, it seems clear that grizzlies could be hunted on a limited basis in some areas. But the public, for the most part, doesn't want *any* grizzly hunting.

3. Sportsmen should have the opportunity to hunt grizzlies, assuming hunters never endanger the bear's existence as a species or even a local population. However, this hunting should be carefully monitored and allowed only after professionals have proved it biologically sound.

4. Considering the number of grizzlies available for harvest, no hunter should ever be allowed to take more than one trophy in his lifetime. The grizzly is indeed "the ultimate trophy," an honor to be spread as thinly as possible among the hunting fraternity.

5. From any viewpoint, it seems logical to let the professionals handle grizzly management. They may not have all the biological information they desire, but they definitely know more about it than anyone else. Game department bear managers don't wish to exterminate the grizzly. They care about the big bear just as much or more than the total protectionist from urban America.

6. Professional management — "harvest type" or "sustained yield" or whatever — often includes sport hunting. Although this aspect of bear management is undesirable from the anti-hunter view, a managed "sustained yield" but stable population, is preferable to an unmanaged, declining population. Management details are unimportant in the face of other serious threats to the bear's survival.

7. An annoying part of the hunting debate is the federal/state argument over who "owns" the bear. For management and liability purposes, the states "own" the grizzly. But nobody "owns" the grizzly. He belongs to the mountain, the meadow, the perilous peaks, to wild nature, to himself. Man isn't worthy or capable of "owning" this majestic creature.

8. A "victory" for the no-hunting forces could lull grizzly supporters into a false sense of complacency concerning the bear's problems. If anyone says, in effect, "We've stopped hunting, so now the grizzly is okay," he has prematurely deserted his cause. In other words, the wilderness king continues to face a variety of threats that require constant attention.

The hunting debate is hardly the primary purpose of this book.

Nevertheless, this question — to hunt or not to hunt — must be addressed because, as John Craighead notes, "You must face the hunting issue because it's so important to so many people."

To conclude, perhaps Jonkel, a foremost authority on grizzlies, put it best when he said, "In some cases, excessive preoccupation with the pros and cons of hunting bears has diverted attention from problems more urgent to the grizzly's preservation."

WHEN MAN AND BEAR MEET

Americans have been influenced by what psychologists call "negative conditioning." And the grizzly is an excellent example. People have been encouraged to view the grizzly as an uncompromising, bloodthirsty man-eater. They've been repeatedly told that the grizzly is a huge, fierce, awesome, vicious beast. Now, they involuntarily believe it.

Mention bears to a pre-school child and expect to hear an exclamation about being "eaten up." Likewise, some adults regret wild lands being "infested" with grizzlies. Even the grizzly's first Latin name, *Ursus horribilis* — "the horrible bear," —reflected this conditioning.[1]

Several noted naturalists partly blame Lewis and Clark and other early explorers for starting this negativism. True, Lewis and Clark thoroughly described the species, thus making a significant contribution to science. But serious grizzly students say the two captains misinterpreted the grizzly's personality. Critics claim that most reported confrontations where bears "charged" were merely close contact with curious grizzlies — bears that didn't recognize white man's strange scent.

The grizzly had only known native Americans with their primitive weapons, not white men with their firearms. Thus, bears probably remained more visible than they do nowadays. After all, they had little need to hide. They could come close to Indians without incident, as the natives avoided the grizzly. But white men saw the big bear as a threat and used their firearms.

Most "white bears" that actually attacked the explorers were those they had wounded with inadequate firearms. Ballistics experts have concluded that early smooth bore rifles definitely didn't have enough wallop to put down a full-grown grizzly.

Unless wounded, the grizzlies observed by Lewis and Clark were, for the most part, not the savage beasts the two captains described. For example,

[1]The Latin name was later changed to *Ursus arctos horribilis*.

grizzlies were so numerous around the present-day city of Great Falls, Montana, the captains forbade anyone to leave camp at night. Realistically, though, if the big bears had lived up to their reputation, they could have moved into camp and easily wiped out the entire expedition.

On June 14, 1804, Lewis shot a buffalo at a considerable distance from the expedition's base camp. While waiting for the animal to die and forgetting to recharge his muzzle loader, "...a large white or reather brown bear, had perceived and crept on me within 20 steps before I discovered him."

Remembering his unloaded firearm, Lewis quickly canvassed the surroundings and discovered there was no tree to climb for at least 300 yards. In desperation, Lewis decided to retreat at a brisk walk, hoping to reach the distant tree. "...But I had no sooner terned myself about but he pitched at me, open mouthed and full speed, I ran about 80 yards and found he gained on me fast, I then run into the water the idea struck me to get into the water to such debth that I could stand and he would be obliged to swim, and that I could in that situation defend myself with my espontoon [a short staff with a steel lance point at the end]....

Lewis ran into the river up to his waist and then turned to face the bear, espontoon in hand. The bear came to the edge of the water, 20 feet away, but no combat followed.

"...The moment I put myself in this attitude of defence he sudonly wheeled about as if frightened, declined to combat on such unequal grounds, and retreated with quite as great precipitation as he had just before pursued me.

"I saw him run through the level open plain about three miles, till he disappeared in the woods on medecine river; during the whole of this distance he ran at full speed, sometimes appearing to look behind him as if he expected pursuit. "[1]

One can make several observations from this experience. First, if the grizzly had indeed been only "20 steps" from Lewis and had come at him with full speed to kill him, either he would have caught Lewis in 80 yards or pursued him into the river.

Second, Lewis went on for a paragraph or so trying to explain the bear's unexpected flight, never arriving at any conclusion. However, he didn't consider the possibility of a curious grizzly merely investigating this strange

[1]DeVoto, Bernard. *The Journals of Lewis and Clark.* Houghton Mifflin Company, Boston, 1953.

white man, most likely the first the bear had ever seen.

Of course, Lewis and Clark were also victims of "negative conditioning." Long before they entered grizzly country, the plains Indians had told them of the "dreadful bear," which the tribes wouldn't attack without at least six warriors. Even then, the bear often won.

Also, at least older grizzlies have poor eyesight, making it difficult for them to distinguish details at 100 yards. So perhaps some of those "charging" grizzlies were merely coming in for a closer look. Andy Russell and his sons spent months filming grizzlies. Several times, the bears bolted right at the Russells, who kept the cameras turning. Without exception, the bear would veer off and flee upon confirming the presence of man.

Three grizzly addicts — Andy Russell, Enos Mills, and William Wright — trailed, observed, hunted, and photographed hundreds of grizzlies, often coming within a few feet of the big bears. Incredibly, Wright took some of the first grizzly pictures with ancient box cameras and flash powder. He would set up his equipment by a well-traveled bear trail at dusk. During the night, when he heard a grizzly coming, he would touch off the flash powder. None of these men carried a gun, nor did any of them need it.

James Capen Adams earned the name "Grizzly" Adams by subduing grizzlies and making them his "house pets." He even rode them and trained them to carry packs.

Granted, these are only a few accounts from men who put their experiences into history by writing books. But anyone who has seriously studied grizzlies will say their savage nature has been exaggerated. In short, professionals insist the infamous, man-killing reputation is nothing but a long-repeated misinterpretation of the grizzly's true personality.

Unfortunately, early writers and orators took the Lewis and Clark journals and repeated, magnified, and glamorized the bear's bad reputation until it became so ingrained in American tradition that today, it's nearly impossible to introduce the real grizzly to a preconditioned public. It's one of those myths that never dies, regardless of attempts to dispel it. Several early naturalists tried unsuccessfully to change public opinion.

Enos Mills, for one, had this to say in his 1919 book *The Grizzly Bear: Our Greatest Wild Animal:* "But is the grizzly bear ferocious? All the first-hand evidence I can find says he is not. Speaking from years of experience with him my answer is emphatically, 'No!' Nearly every one whom a grizzly has killed went out with the special intention of killing a grizzly. The majority of people who hold the opinion that he is not ferocious are those who have studied him without attempting to kill him; while the majority who say that he is ferocious are those who have killed or attempted to kill him.

"During the greater part of my life I have lived in a grizzly bear region. I have camped for months alone and without a gun in their territory. I have seen them when alone and when with hunters, in Colorado, Utah, Arizona, Mexico, Wyoming, Montana, Idaho, Washington, British Columbia, and Alaska. I have spent weeks trailing and watching grizzlies, and their tracks in the snow showed that they often trailed me. They frequently came close, and there were times when they might have attacked me with every advantage. But they did not do so. As they never made any attack on me, nor on any one else that I know of who was not bent on killing them, I can only conclude that they are not ferocious."

"Are grizzlies man killers?" asks Andy Russell, who should know if anybody does. "I would have to say no. But occasionally one breaks the rule for one reason or another....If the grizzly bear were half as bad as commonly portrayed, early explorers and frontiersmen would not have gotten far across the prairies, and the opening of the West would likely have been delayed until the advent of repeating rifles."

It would be possible to fill many pages with authoritative opinion saying the grizzly's ferocity has been overstated. But such documentation probably wouldn't end negative attitudes toward the big bear — not as long as people can recall a single bloody meeting between bear and man. And the press will keep people informed, as grizzly maulings have high news value. The backpacker who hikes all his life without seeing a grizzly makes no news.

What about the recent deaths in the national parks? Specifically, two young women were killed in Montana's Glacier Park in 1967, a young man in Yellowstone Park in 1972, a young woman in Canada's Glacier Park in 1976, a young man in Alaska's Glacier Bay National Monument in 1976, and another young woman in Montana's Glacier Park in 1976.

From its establishment in 1910 to 1967, Montana's Glacier Park had gone without a grizzly-caused fatality. Suddenly, on August 13, 1967, two different grizzlies attacked two young women, Michele Koons and Julie Helgeson, in separated locations at almost exactly the same time. It was, at the least, a gigantic coincidence and nearly a statistical impossibility. It was also a tragedy that ignited a fierce controversy.

When this catastrophe occurred, I was working in Glacier and had a front row seat for the following debate which produced these facts:

● Both bears were accustomed to feeding on human garbage. In one case (Granite Park), the garbage was deliberately placed so tourists could view the grizzlies when they came to feed. The campground was within 200 yards of this garbage dump. Park officials knew about the garbage situation, but failed to do anything about it even though it violated park policy. Also, the park had been warned by wildlife experts to correct the situation to avoid serious trouble.

• In the other case (Trout Creek), an obviously "bad" grizzly had been terrorizing cabins and campgrounds within the park. Campers and park residents had asked the park to do something about the bear. About a week before the woman was killed at Trout Creek Campground, a troop of Girl Scouts had frantically fled this same campground as a grizzly tore apart their camp. This incident had been covered in the local newspaper.

• One woman was menstruating and the other was expecting her menstrual period, according to the park's report on the incident. Park handouts and trail head signs warn females against entering grizzly country during menstrual periods.

• Park bears are completely protected from hunters and predator control. Thus, according to many authorities, the bears have become less wary of man than bears in nonpark areas where they are hunted.

In retrospect, park officials should have acted quickly in the face of an obvious life-threatening situation. They should have killed the bad bears and closed the garbage dumping immediately. Even a temporary action — closing certain campgrounds and trails — might have prevented the tragedy.

In fairness to park officials, 1967 was a trying year for Glacier's administrators. When these incidents occurred, the park had about 40 wildfires burning within its boundaries. Because the NPS budget has not kept up with the public's demand for park services, Glacier lacked adequate professional staffing to cover every emergency.

In Yellowstone, some of the same general circumstances brought the death of a young male camper in 1972. Although no litigation resulted from the 1967 Glacier Park fatalities, the 1972 death in Yellowstone brought legal action. The victim's parents took the NPS to court and, in turn, received $87,417.67 in damages. In addition, Federal Court Judge A. Andrew Hauk castigated park officials for not following the Craigheads' recommendations and "thus negligently creating an unreasonable danger to park visitors."

The NPS, through its parent agency, the U.S. Department of the Interior, appealed this decision to a higher court. Here, the decision was overturned.

After these incidents, both parks improved information campaigns to educate visitors about bears and enacted "preventive management" plans bent on avoiding confrontations. After any suspicious incident, trails — even entire drainages — were closed immediately. "We closed 40 trails last year [1975] alone," Chuck Sigler, chief park ranger at Glacier, recalls.

Some campgrounds and trails were moved from areas of high grizzly use. And a strict "pack in, pack out" policy went into effect. This policy, which requires hikers and campers to carry out everything they carry in, has been successful in reducing the amount of human garbage left in grizzly country.

But preventive management didn't prevent a night of terror for five female campers on September 23, 1976. And one of them isn't alive to complain.

Five University of Montana co-eds had come to the Many Glacier area on the east side of Montana's Glacier Park eager for an autumn backpack trip. However, finding their trail closed because of a "bear incident," they pitched their small tents in the vehicle campground and turned in.

About 7:00 a.m., a bear tore into one of the tents, clawing at the closest camper, 22-year-old Mary Pat Mahoney, and then retreated. Seconds later, the bear returned and amid wild screaming dragged Mahoney away and killer her.

Had the Park Service let dust gather on vital policies? Or was this a "statistic waiting to happen," as Clifford Martinka, head of wildlife and research at Glacier, puts it? Consider these facts:

• The young women were well-informed. Before making camp, they had asked park rangers about the bear situation at least twice.

• Their camp was immaculate — no food or garbage problems. They had locked extra food in the trunk of their car. That evening, they had prepared a meatless meal as an additional precaution.

• The women weren't menstruating, nor did they use hair spray, perfume, or other strong-smelling cosmetics.

• The attack wasn't provoked in any way, as in many past encounters where somebody moved between a female and her young or startled a bear.

• Grizzlies in the area had tasted human food and garbage by ransacking packs and camps earlier that summer. But nobody knows positively whether these were the same bears involved in the Mahoney incident.

• The seasonal ranger in charge of the area had acted as outlined by the park's bear management plan. He had closed the trails where confrontations had occurred. In fact, almost the entire drainage was closed except for the drive-in campground.

"I think Reese [the ranger] followed the book [the bear management plan] very adequately," Jonkel, who sat on the Board of Inquiry that

69

investigated the incident, notes. "The problem was the book didn't provide for an atypical situation like this. I would not have camped there if I had been told what these girls were told — and especially after the incidents earlier that week. But then I have special knowledge of bears which the girls, the seasonal ranger, or most other people, do not have."

Jonkel is referring to several minor incidents that occurred in the two weeks preceding the fatal confrontation. Specifically, two fishermen — who hadn't provoked the bears in any way — were chased, two or three camps were ransacked, and the day before the fatal attack, two grizzlies walked through the vehicle campground.

After the calamity, the Park Service received the usual criticism from an irate few. But was the Park Service — or anybody else, for that matter — at fault?

Park officials have been sincere in their attempts to make the parks as safe as possible. Granted, bear management hasn't been perfect, and hindsight is always sharper than foresight. However, the park should have prepared for the extreme situation where a grizzly might come into a developed campground. It's a safe bet that future bear management plans will outline procedures for vehicle campground closures, a policy which would have saved Mahoney's life. Unfortunately, it usually takes a tragedy to prompt long-needed action.

"This probably was predictable," Martinka admits. "But we weren't ready for it. There's got to be a way to predict these things."

Actually, in 1969, Jack Olsen, author of *The Night of the Grizzlies,* predicted Mary Pat Mahoney's death. In his book about the two fatal maulings in 1967, he wrote, "A summer or two, perhaps three or four, may pass without serious injury. But inevitably standards will slip, complacency and human error will return, and along will come another grizzly that is peculiar...or another grizzly that has been baited into proximity with humans and lost its respect and fear.... Then more human life will be sacrificed, almost as certainly as tamaracks lose their needles and beavers eat aspen bark."

But the "standards" really didn't slip this time. If anything, they were strongly in force on September 23, 1976 at Many Glacier. Olsen was warning people that the park administrators would "forget" and allow another obvious life-threatening situation to develop like they did in 1967. But such wasn't the case at Many Glacier. Something else happened, and many people wish they knew what it was.

The long-lived, often-repeated melodrama of man and bear has many faces — anguish, fear, anger, hate, love, excitement, awe, apology, sadness, tragedy, carelessness, irresponsibility, and foolishness. But now there's a new element — mystery.

"This takes it off into a different realm," Ted Sudia, chief scientist for the NPS in Washington, D.C., concedes. "I don't think anybody can explain why the bear attacked this particular woman."

In other cases, inquirers could lay the blame on some specific fault — either of the bear manager or victim. But not this time. "This is the first case that I know of in the lower states that a grizzly came into a tent and attacked people without provocation," Dr. Richard Knight, another bear authority who sat on the Board of Inquiry, said. "We are at a loss," explained the leader of the Inter-agency Grizzly Bear Study Team from the Yellowstone Park area; "they [the campers] did everything right."

"There is nothing in our preliminary investigation to give us a clue as to why they were singled out," echoes Chief Park Naturalist, Ed Rothfuss, who also sat on the Board of Inquiry. "We just don't know why it hit that campground, that campsite, that girl."

However, the most confused of all are the surviving campers who were so careful. "That bear could have picked any tent in the area," one of them remarked in an interview in the *Missoulian,* a daily newspaper of Missoula, Montana. "...I remember thinking this can't be happening to us. We can always remove ourselves from the statistics. But then, we became a statistic."

The Board of Inquiry determined the campers had "followed or exceeded precautions one would normally take," according to Glacier Park Superintendent, Phillip Iverson. "It's like the victim who gets hit by a drunken driver."

The official report of the Board of Inquiry concluded that:

• Park employees had correctly followed the bear management plan.

• Since they had displayed aggressive and abnormal behavior, the two grizzlies were justifiably killed even if they weren't responsible for Mahoney's death.

• Granted, the bear management plan didn't specifically address problems in developed campgrounds. However, the report states, "This is understandable since this is the first such incident to occur in a major campground." Future plans should address management of developed areas.

• Stiffer penalties for illegal camping and carelessness with food may help force compliance with regulations and, in turn, reduce bear/man confrontations.

• Research is needed on the population dynamics of park grizzlies.

• "People-bear encounters were more numerous in Glacier and in the Many Glacier area this year than in any previous year. With increasing visitation in the park, bears encounter more people along the trails and thus may become more aggressive. This trend can be expected to continue creating more management problems and possibly more incidents."

• The location of some facilities was poorly planned, e.g. along major bear routes. Such facilities could be fenced, bypassed with vegetative or fenced corridors, or removed.

• Because the grizzly is listed as a threatened species under the U.S. Endangered Species Act, managers "...have a tendency to react less readily to removing a bum or rogue bear." Total protection may be okay for threatened butterflies, the report stated, but grizzlies — especially in areas used by man — "must be managed. If, through the implementation of the [Endangered] Species Act, we become overly protective of an animal such as the grizzly to the point that incidents and maulings do occur, public sentiment for protection could be lost and in effect, [be] counterproductive to the survival of the species. Good bear management (which includes timely removal of problem bears) is essential to keep the bears in high public regard."

However, the four survivors of the Mahoney incident didn't completely agree. So they sent the following letter to Glacier Park officials.

We are the four women who survived the grizzly bear attack on Sept. 23, 1976, when Mary Patricia Mahoney was killed at Many Glacier Campground in Glacier National Park. At that time and because of recent disclosures, we feel that the Park Service was negligent in informing campers of the hazardous conditions and in taking practical steps to ensure campers' safety.

We particularly question the following aspects of the Service's policy:

1. The poor communication between park personnel and the public between the main gates to the entrances of West Glacier and St. Mary.

When we arrived at the Park on Sept. 22, around 3 p.m. at the West Glacier entrance, we asked the ranger on duty if any trails or campgrounds were closed (since it was the end of the season) and, specifically, if the trails to Swiftcurrent and Iceberg Lakes were open. We were told that both were open.

72

Incorrect information — which in the least is a major inconvenience for visitors to the Park who have a specific destination in mind — should not be given out. We would not have traveled to the Many Glacier Campground if we had been informed that the trails were closed and particularly if we had known they had been closed because of bears.

2. *The vague and incomplete information dispensed by Ranger Fred Reese in informing campers of the dangers.*

When we arrived at Many Glacier Campground at about 5:30 p.m., we drove to the Swiftcurrent and Iceberg Lakes' trailheads finding a sign taped on the board informing us that the trails had been closed due to a "bear incident."

We sought out Reese, who was eating dinner, to inquire about the safety of the area. Reese told us the "bear incidents" involved "young, adolescent bears" getting into people's packs who had not tied up their food in a tree correctly and by people illegally camping, implying that the "incident" or food stealing was the fault of the campers.

We were told that the trail to Grinnell Glacier was open and that it would be safe to go there the next day if we would just "hoot and holler." Reese also told us that he had been camping in the area for "12 years" and had "never had a problem."

We feel that the preceding comments relate to a general everyday situation but did not relate specifically to the situation at hand. Therefore, a realistic appraisal taking into consideration what had been happening in that campground at that time was not given.

Subsequently, we have discovered that the bears — which have been sighted five times in nine days — had made "atypical attacks."

The incidents in which very aggressive behavior was exhibited by grizzlies in the area took place on September 14, 17, 19 (the two adolescents were seen twice on this day) and 22.

The fact that campers' and hikers' safety was threatened was particularly obvious from the incidents of Sept. 19. The adolescent grizzlies entered the Many Glacier campground itself, rummaged through "bear proof" garbage cans and then proceeded directly to Fishercap Lake, which is only .2 of a mile from the Many Glacier Campground. At Fishercap Lake two men who were treed by the grizzlies narrowly escaped serious injury, according to the transcripts from the Board of Inquiry.

During an earlier incident the bears, instead of having their territory or food source threatened, had seen campers from a distance and, instead of retreating, ran towards the campers, who dropped their gear, and ran to safety. The bears then got into their food.

Moreover, an incident occurring during late July in which a grizzly

73

ripped apart a tent in the Many Glacier Campground to get at a sleeping bag and then dragged the shredded bag down to the creek area illustrated weeks in advance of Sept. 23 that the exact method of attack had been learned.

Clear and present danger to the campers' and hikers' lives had been established and it is inexcusable that closure of the area to anything but hard-side camping did not take place.

Furthermore, the term "adolescent bears" used by the ranger gives the person having little or no experience with bears the impression that such bears are not dangerous. In fact, they are among the most dangerous of grizzly bears, because they are attempting to stake out their own territory, are exploring and constantly kept in a stressful situation by other older bears protecting their own territories. Moreover, an "adolescent" bear may weigh 250 pounds, if not more.

We would not have stayed in the area had we been informed of the above information.

3. *The ranger not stating explicitly that the bears in question were grizzlies and in not informing us of the immense strength and capriciousness of grizzly bears.*

We have subsequently learned that the advice Reese gave us of "make certain you put your food in the trunk and everything should be all right" was tremendously insufficient. Grizzlies in fact have the strength to break into a trunk as easily as "into a can of beans," according to Research Scientist Charles Jonkel of the University of Montana in Missoula.

4. *Not closing off the area in which a bear trap is set.*

We were under the impression that the trap had been set in the area, but we have subsequently come to believe the trap was set in the portion of the campground that was "closed off" by sawhorses.

What if we had driven into the area at 2 a.m. and had not seen the signs and had camped right next to the trap?

It has subsequently been reported to us that an acquaintance of ours inadvertently camped adjacent to the trap about a week before us and had not been notified of the trap being set.

5. *The understaffing of the campground.*

There was only one ranger, Reese, on duty in an area that had had problems with bears. Fortunately, a vacationing ranger from California at the campground aided Reese in the killing of the bears under suspicion. (The other resident ranger was away at a training school.) This is in particular reference to Subdistrict Ranger, Lloyd Kortge's

74

statement in the transcripts that he and Reese had seriously considered tranquilizing the problem grizzlies but were unable to do so because of lack of personnel.

6. *Allowing people to go into the area before a thorough investigation and determination was made via a post mortem examination of the bears that were killed to ensure that they were indeed the bears responsible for Mahoney's death.*

As we were leaving, a backpacker was engaged in a conversation with Reese, who was trying to dissuade him from hiking in the area, but who also told the man that he was "99 percent sure" that the problem bears had been shot.

Newspaper reports now show that the young bears that were shot were not necessarily responsible for the fatal mauling, and, therefore, a thorough investigation before opening the area in question for even daytime usage should have been undertaken.

We strongly recommend strict adherence to a Park management plan that would ensure:

1. Distribution at all entrances of the Park of current and accurate information about open or closed trails.

2. Complete distribution of accurate and specific information about "typical and atypical" bear behavior relating to the situation at hand.

All the times and locations of bear sightings in the area should be stated to campers and hikers. Campgrounds and trails in proximity to bears known to have exhibited "atypical behavior" should be sealed off until reasonable safety can be assured by means of trapping and evacuation of the problem grizzly or grizzlies.

3. Identification of the type of bears sighted in an area (i.e., grizzly and/or black bears).

For example, if sightings were of grizzlies, campers should be told of the general strength, size, intelligence, known behavior, attractants and deterrents of grizzlies. Campers should also be informed of the ability of grizzlies to penetrate the protection of automobile shelters.

4. Notification of the existence and exact locations of traps by way of diagrammatic bulletins posted at the ranger stations, campsites, restrooms and trailheads.

The reasons for the necessity of the traps should also be stated.

If an area is closed off because of a trap setting, this should be clearly stated in boldface printing (as in a large poster).

5. Complete staffing of all areas of the Park open to the public. Late in the season if the staff size has been decreased, less popular areas of the Park should be closed for recreational use to enable maximum

safety in the areas that are open.

6.   That in an area where a fatality from a bear mauling has resulted the area should be immediately sealed off to hikers and campers until a thorough investigation is completed.

7.   That if the "atypical behavior" of grizzly and/or black bears can be attributed to the massive increase in the number of visitors and the concomitant decrease in the available range for the bear population, then two courses of action should be considered:

(1)   The number of visitors should be limited by using a reservation system allowing fewer numbers of people to visit the Park a season.

(2)   Hunting of grizzlies and other Park bears should be allowed until the number of bears is compatible with the available land area and the number of people using the Park.

8.   Improve the quality of pamphlets and educational materials distributed to Park visitors to better inform them about bears and related hazards.

We would like an immediate reply to this letter (within 10 days).

> Sincerely,
> Jennifer Thompson
> Ellen Fineman
> Barbara Tucker
> Patricia Tucker

To the survivers' lengthy letter, Superintendent Iverson replied, "I appreciate the comments and suggestions offered in your letter. Your recommendations indicate that you have given a considerable amount of careful thought to the bear-visitor relationship in Glacier National Park. We certainly will give your input genuine consideration."

There are some questions that fade into history unanswered, and what was responsible for the death of Mary Pat Mahoney may be one of them. And the all-important question of whether grizzlies are too dangerous still lingers.

A million or so tourists flock to Glacier Park every year. Since 1913, 135 persons have died in the park from causes other than bear maulings: 27 in falls while hiking or climbing, 17 in vehicle accidents, 36 from drowning, and 55 from various causes ranging from avalanches to hypothermia. During the same time, grizzlies killed only three people, 2 in 1967 and 1 in 1976. Meanwhile, over 27 million people have visited Glacier.

76

In Yellowstone, about four persons die each year in vehicle accidents, a fall claims someone every five years; and one person drowns every year. Comparing these averages with deaths from grizzly maulings paints a similar picture to the one in Glacier. Since the park was created in 1872, only three persons (one each in 1906, 1916, and 1972) have been killed by grizzlies. Total visitation figures aren't available, but somewhere around 60 million tourists have visited Yellowstone.

In 1970, after the untimely deaths of the two young women in Glacier Park in 1967, Dr. Stephen Herrero of the University of Calgary (Alberta) covered the bear/man relationship in a technical and comprehensive article in *Science,* a magazine written for and by scientists. Herrero called the probability of getting mauled by a grizzly "negligible" — something like .00007%. "During the almost 100-year history of North American national parks that harbor the grizzly there have been a minimum of 150 million visitors," he wrote. "Only 77 persons have been injured by grizzly bears in 66 separate incidents. This gives an injury rate of about 1 person per 2 million visitors. The death rate is 1 person per 30 million visitors. This may be compared to 1.9 million human beings injured in motor vehicle accidents in the United States during 1967. This was about 1 percent of the total population of the United States, or 1 out of 100 people."

Somehow, such statistical analysis — although it puts the situation in perspective — does little to allay the concern of millions of Americans. Any statistician can conclude that the chance of grizzly trouble is immeasurably slim. Bees and wasps, lightning, motor vehicles, and cigarette smoking kill many more people than grizzly bears do. Indeed, a good researcher would probably discover — to the dismay of many pet owners — that domestic dogs kill and maim more people than grizzly bears do. But this numbers game seems irrelevant — no matter how remote the probability, it merely means the bad number is sure to come up sooner or later, as it did on September 23, 1976 for Mary Pat Mahoney.

In recent history, bloody meetings between bear and man have been almost totally restricted to the national parks. In 1956, Kenneth Scott from Fort Benton, Montana wounded a grizzly while hunting the Bob Marshall Wilderness. Then the injured bear turned on Scott and killed him. Except for this incident, however, searches of game department and historical society files failed to turn up another grizzly-caused mortality south of Canada in a *nonpark* area. There have been two or three nonfatal maulings, but not a single one serious enough to cause death.

In these nonpark areas, grizzlies avoid man partly because hunting is still

77

The grizzly is dangerous. But how dangerous? Too dangerous to allow the bears to roam wild and free in the national parks where thousands of hikers also roam wild and free? Doug O'looney photo.

Hikers in Montana's Glacier National Park and a few other American and Canadian parks face many hazards, including the threat of a bear mauling. Do wilderness hikers want total safety? Bill Schneider photo.

allowed or has been until recently. Here, the bears associate man with danger, not with food. After decades of being pursued, the grizzly has learned to outwit hunters and, at the same time, avoid all humans. Ask any hunter who has tried to bag a trophy grizzly. Successful or unsuccessful, he will undoubtedly mutter something about "the greatest challenge" or "smartest animal in the world." In his 1910 book, *The Grizzly Bear,* William Wright told of a hunter who commented that if he saw 50 grizzly tracks for every deer track that he would be guaranteed to bag 6 deer without seeing a single silvertip.

Old Eph is a wise old bear. He knows when and where he's safe. Outside the parks, hunters still stalk him. But once across the invisible park boundary, he's not pursued. In the parks, he's the dominant species, and he knows it. There, he has grown accustomed to man. Or worse, he may be growing steadily *more* accustomed to man, a trend with a guaranteed disastrous ending.

The level of human use also partly accounts for the scarcity of bear/man encounters outside the parks. Most parks experience intensive recreational use which makes confrontations more statistically probable. But worse, it often helps create that individual "rogue" bear which, according to John Craighead, is responsible for many maulings.

More people usually means more garbage. And even with good sanitation, grizzlies still get food in the presence of man. This means bears begin to associate man with food, not with danger. This can create a dangerous, or as John Craighead puts it, "man-conditioned," grizzly, which has probably been responsible for most maulings in the parks.

Conversely, nonpark grizzly habitat has fewer hikers and campers, so grizzlies rarely get food from man. Thus, grizzly country outside the parks has fewer bear/man encounters.

To help make the parks safer, the Park Service will undoubtedly cut back on human use in some areas like the Many Glacier valley, where wilderness travel (particularly day use) has mushroomed. Perhaps there is some unknown level of human intrusion that grizzlies can't tolerate. And when that level of tolerance is crossed, when there are too many humans using grizzly country, the result may be most unsavory.

Biologists almost universially agree on the need for reduced human use of grizzly habitat. However, they aren't sure such action is enough, especially *if* the grizzly population is gradually becoming less wary of man.

The parks are preserves where hunting isn't allowed, as it is in the national forests. Somehow, park bears must be kept wary. Only then can fewer

Statistically, campers in grizzly country outside the national parks have a smaller chance of an ugly bear/man confrontation. Most grizzly maulings occur within the national parks. Bill Schneider photos.

confrontations be expected.

Wildlife managers like this idea, but they have failed to come up with a workable and socially acceptable method. To the game departments and some sportsmen, regulated hunting in the parks represents an acceptable solution. But this stands little chance of political approval.

Researchers have experimented with deterrent drugs such as lithium chloride that won't kill a bear, but will make it violently ill. If a successful deterrent drug is found, rangers could set bait for bears and thus train them to avoid people and garbage. After many years — perhaps it will take several generations — the park bears may fear man, as in ages past, reinstating a trait that surely contributed to their survival into modern times.

Electrical shock "traps" set up around baits or campgrounds are another possibility. Or, as Jonkel puts it, "Shoot them with rock salt — or whatever." Regardless of the method, the grizzly must be made painfully aware of man.

In addition to teaching the bear, "we have to make people smarter, too," Jonkel suggests. To make people follow "the rules," he recommends $200-300 fines for such violations as illegal camping or leaving food in the backcountry.

Some scientists suspect such solutions aren't practical and because of the incalculably high value of human life, have advocated eliminating the grizzly from the national parks to make them safer for people. Shortly after the two 1967 fatalities in Glacier Park (1968 and 1969), Gairdner B. Moment from Goucher College, Baltimore, Maryland, suggested ridding Glacier and Yellowstone of the grizzly and restricting the bear to nonpark habitat that doesn't have as much attraction for hiking and other outdoor pursuits as the parks.

Moment's articles stirred up biologists, most of whom rose to the grizzly's defense. They criticized Moment's stand and emphasized the need to preserve the grizzly as part of natural systems found only in the national parks. They also pointed out that bear research wasn't Moment's area of expertise. Of the defenders, Herrero, who has extensively studied bears, was especially ardent. In 1970, he replied to Moment with a follow-up article in *BioScience*.

"[Several] outstanding biologists including Charles Darwin have presented the case for preserving maximum diversity in our remaining natural areas," Herrero wrote. "They argue convincingly that one way in which the diversity of people and their behaviors is well served is by offering the widest possible range of experience in nature. There is no doubt that grizzly populations in Glacier and Yellowstone can serve this role.

"In deciding the value of the grizzly in these circumstances, we must look beyond the present and into the future. With increasing urbanization and automation, man will become even more removed from nature, and the contrast and stimulation offered by the wilderness experience will be even greater....To many people the grizzly symbolizes wilderness, makes it come alive in both our minds and our hearts. To exist and explore safely in grizzly country is an experience through which men may find significant dimensions of themselves.

"If relatively undisturbed museums of natural history cannot exist in National Parks, then where will they survive?" Herrero asked, "If we lose the grizzly bear in our National Parks, we will have lost another degree of freedom, yet another choice and challenge, and in so doing we may find ourselves adrift from our history, our design, and ourselves."

Even some victims of grizzly maulings won't accept Moment's theory. Robert Hahm, who was mauled while trying to photograph a female grizzly and her cubs in Glacier in 1968, had this to say: "The thing that makes me very unhappy about the whole incident is my fear that this will only add fuel to the fire for those people who advocate the destruction of the grizzly to make our national parks safe. There is no reason, in the name of civilized progress, to kill an animal for doing what is natural," Hahm pleads. "I feel no malice toward the bear. It was my fault for sticking my neck out too far — the bear was only protecting her young and her territory. The only thing that will prevent me from hiking in the wilderness again is the eventual destruction of that wilderness itself, and when anyone advocates the destruction of grizzlies, he is in essence advocating the destruction of the true wilderness. Let us pray that this never happens."

After serious injury or death occurs, the "problem bear" is usually destroyed. Occasionally, more than one bear is shot, as rangers rarely know for sure which bear is the culprit until an autopsy is performed.

In 1976, a female grizzly killed a young woman in Canada's Glacier Park. Soon thereafter, authorities shot the she-bear and her three cubs. After the incident in September, 1976 in Montana's Glacier Park, two young grizzlies were shot, but authorities were never sure they had brought down the killer.

Is this revenge justified? If not, what should authorities do in the aftermath of a tragedy?

Generally, man is the intruder. Often, the grizzly merely acts in self defense. When a human kills another animal or even another human in self defense, all is forgiven. But park managers don't forgive Old Ephraim for acting in self defense. They, in their words, "remove him from the population.''

This punishment has public relations benefits, as people get the impression corrective action has been taken promptly. Most likely, the public would adversely react to the Park Service permitting a killer bear to go free — perhaps to kill again. In many cases, a bad bear will stay bad. Thus, his removal may prevent future confrontations.

Some preservationists worry about killing even one individual in a threatened animal population. In the Glacier Park situation, however, removing a few problem bears has little impact on the park's grizzly population, according to Dr. Charles Jonkel. If anything it has a positive impact by removing surplus bears, as most biologists, including Jonkel, suspect Glacier and other parks are overpopulated with grizzlies.

In the case of cubs, they may have gained a dangerous bit of knowledge by watching their mother kill a human. Also, they may die a slow death if they're forced into the wild without their mother. Likewise, the logic of capturing cubs so they can spend the rest of their days in zoos is suspect.

Finally, killing bad grizzlies may help make the entire population more wary of man. This, of course, actually improves the species' chances for survival.

Actually, after researching the competitive relationship between man and bear, it's difficult to explain why there are so *few* maulings. Here is an animal weighing 400-800 pounds with the speed of a greyhound — truly a picture of power and unpredictability.

In the parks, thousands — *indeed, hundreds of thousands* — of hikers swarm into every nook and cranny of grizzly country every year. Still, there are amazingly few confrontations, even though the grizzly could kill these recreationists as easily as man swats flies.

In 1967, about two weeks after the two women were mauled to death, I was fighting one of Glacier Park's forest fires. The fire line we were checking that day dipped into a steep, brush-filled gully. At the bottom, we heard an ominous rustling in the nearby thicket. "Just a squirrel" my partner shrugged.

About 100 yards up the hill, more noise in the ravine prompted quick glances over our shoulders. There, standing exactly where we had been about one minute earlier was a large, skinny-looking grizzly. We had passed within 15 or 20 feet of the hiding bear. If the silvertip is a man killer, how can the big bear resist such easy prey?

Without doubt, the grizzly is unpredictable. "The longer I live," Andy Russell notes, "the more I hesitate to state firmly that grizzlies do or do not do

84

certain things. As surely as one does, some grizzly comes along to refute the words of profound wisdom.''

When attacked, cornered (or when he *thinks* he's cornered) or when a female grizzly considers her cubs endangered, the big bear can be devastating. In the late 19th Century, bear/bull fight promoters matched a grizzly with an African lion — ''the King of Beasts.'' The lion lasted about long enough for the crowd to get a single breath. Certainly a human being wouldn't have lasted even that long. Yes, the grizzly has the physical and mental characteristics of a very dangerous wild animal. But is he?

John Craighead uses the unscientific cliche — ''about the same chance of getting hit by lightning as getting mauled by a grizzly.'' But this tired adage can help illustrate how dangerous grizzly country really is.

If somebody wants to get hit by lightning, he runs around on a ridge during a thunderstorm with a lightning rod in one hand and an electric appliance in the other. If he wants to get mauled by a grizzly, he sneaks around wilderness trails trying to surprise a slumbering silvertip, carries perishable food and spreads it around his campsite, or moves between a female grizzly and her cubs. The point is — *if wilderness users follow a few simple rules grizzly country is very safe.* [1]

''Clearly, it is possible to pass long periods of time, on foot, in grizzly country, without injury, as the Craigheads in their 11-year study of the grizzly have shown,'' Herrero observes. ''This suggests that knowledge of the grizzlies' habits, coupled with an understanding of wilderness travel can enhance but not guarantee total safety. Do wilderness travelers want or need total safety?''

Even with the strictest wilderness ethics and manners, there will be future confrontations. As long as man and grizzly occupy the same space, there will be a few tragic encounters. The chance might be one in several million, but there's still an undeniable risk.

The spirit of the wilderness is embodied in this magnificent mammal. Therefore, backcountry enthusiasts could consider the remote chance of confrontating a grizzly as ''part of the deal'' — just like runaway forest fires, flash floods, falling trees, landslides, adverse weather, and lightning. If someone doesn't like the odds of encountering a grizzly, he can go to an eastern wild land where Old Ephraim has never ranged or to a western wilderness where the big bear has been exterminated. In these western

[1] Refer to a list of basic rules in this chapter. Also, a complete set can be picked up at many National Park Service and Forest Service offices.

GRIZZLY COUNTRY MANNERS[1]

General Rules

- Be cautious and alert. Look around as you hike. Grizzlies can sometimes be spotted in open areas a good distance away. Stay together.

- Never hike in grizzly country alone.

- Watch for bear sign and be extra cautious when you find it.

- Leave your dog home. Your pet may be "man's best friend" at home, but not in the wilderness where he could attract a grizzly.

- Report all grizzly incidents to local authorities.

Hiking

- If you see a grizzly at a distance, make a wide detour on the upwind side so the bear can get your scent. If a detour isn't possible, slowly back down the trail until safely out of sight. Then, make lots of noise (the more, the better) and slowly and noisily make your way up the trail again. The bear should be gone when you get back to your earlier observation point. If the bear is still there and you can't safely get around him, abandon your trip.

[1]Keep in mind these are merely general rules. They're probably the best generalities anywhere, but as always, it's dangerous to generalize. Certainly, there is no concrete formula for avoiding confrontations or for what to do when you are confronted. Dr. Charles Jonkel, upon reviewing these rules, suggested trying to evaluate each individual situation based on these general rules. And by all means, Jonkel emphasized, "try to avoid an encounter."

• Although it isn't a foolproof method, making noise while hiking helps avoid bears. Many hikers hang bells or a can of pebbles from their packs or belts. As a general rule, the noisier, the safer. Metallic noise seems more effective than human voices which can be muffled by natural conditions. Also, it's difficult to keep up steady conversation during long hikes.

Camping

• Be careful and neat with food and garbage. Keep a clean camp.

• Don't camp in sites obviously frequented by bears. If you see a bear or fresh sign where you intended to camp, pick another campsite.

• If possible, camp near tall trees that can be easily climbed.

• Sleep some distance from your campfire and cooking area.

• Keep food and garbage out of reach of bears at night (such as suspended between two trees) and away from your sleeping area. Keep food odors off clothes, tents, and sleeping bags. Avoid fresh, perishable, or "smelly" foods.

• Burn combustible trash if regulations allow open fires. Burn cans and other incombustibles to remove odors. Then, dig them out of the ashes and pack them out. Never bury trash in the backcountry. If you can carry it in, you can carry it out.

• If you fish, be careful when cleaning them. Burn fish entrails, if possible. Never leave them around camp. Fish can attract bears. Camping at popular fishing sites requires extra caution.

Special Precautions For Women

● Stay out of grizzly country during menstrual periods.

● Avoid using perfume, hair spray, deodorants, or other cosmetics. There is some evidence that bears are attracted and even infuriated by these scents.

The Confrontation

● Most important, try to remain calm. Never panic and run. You can't outrun a grizzly. And by rapid retreat, you may excite the bear into pursuit.

● If the bear stands his ground and doesn't seem aggressive, stand still. Don't move toward the bear. Start looking for a tree to climb. And if the grizzly moves toward you, get up it fast. Make sure it's tall enough to get you out of reach. (Only grizzly cubs can climb trees.) Before starting for the tree, drop something like a pack or camera to possibly distract the bear. Stay up the tree until you're positive the bear has moved out of the area.

● If the grizzly continues his unaggressive behavior, back very slowly and quietly down the trail until out of sight.

● If you can't get up a tree, play dead. Curl up and clasp your hands over the back of your neck in the "cannonball" position. Grizzlies have often bypassed or only slightly injured people in this position. This takes courage, to say the least, but it's preferable to serious injury.

● Physical resistance is, of course, useless.

areas, however, the wilderness isn't quite complete; it's missing its most outstanding inhabitant, the grizzly.

"The underprivileged urbanite may or may not believe my data...on the infrequent occurrence of attacks, but even this [remote chance of bear trouble] will seem too great a risk to them if one of us does not convey the magic, love, mystery, and wildness that the grizzly can embody," Herrero notes. "For a person who neither loves nor understands the grizzly any risk of injury is too great."

Herrero and many others would apparently take the chance because of the richer experience they receive just knowing the great white bear is "out there" somewhere. The sight of those massive, clawed tracks pressed into the mud or snow adds a new dimension to the wilderness experience. Just knowing they are sharing the mountain with the king of the American wilderness is a royal privilege and a moving adventure like no other.

Realizing the grizzly's true nature is vital to preserving the species. If people won't tolerate the grizzly, he doesn't have a chance. If they can't shed, or at least ease, their fears, efforts to increase or stabilize the bear population will suffer.

Regrettably, misrepresentations of the grizzly's character negate efforts to gain this level of understanding. Instead of allaying fear and hatred, some writers and film makers exploit it by playing on common conceptions of grizzly bears, sharks, and other large predators, thus worsening the situation. And recent books and movies entitled *Grizzly* and *Jaws* provide excellent examples.

In the case of *Grizzly*, the title was perhaps the most original part of the movie produced by Film Ventures International. *Grizzly* was a sequel (or perhaps more appropriately, an imitation) of *Jaws*, a money-making hit based on Peter Benchley's novel. The press kit for *Grizzly* billed the star as 2,000 pounds and "18 feet of gut-crunching, man-eating terror."

Apparently, movie makers race to get on the coattails of a winner, as at least one other film company was working on a sequel to *Jaws* about a grizzly.[1] But it must be demoralizing not using original movie ideas, let alone not being able to do an acceptable job of copying somebody else's idea.

In *Jaws*, an oversized shark mysteriously appears in the shallow waters off a resort community. After the killer shark has attacked several swimmers,

---

[1] American International Pictures had begun producing a movie called *Claws* which reportedly had a similar plot to *Grizzly*. However, Film Ventures International brought its movie out first, so American International Pictures dropped its plans.

The sight of those massive, clawed tracks pressed in the snow or mud adds a new and exhilarating dimension to the wilderness experience. Rick Trembath photo.

the local sheriff, the "hero," tries to close the beach. However, the town leaders, worried about the local economy, talk him out of it. After a few more swimmers have been torn to pieces, the beach is finally closed, and the hero and two others go shark hunting. After the shark attacks their boat and sinks it, the sheriff ends up floating on a piece of debris with, luckily, a high powered rifle. When the shark comes for him, the sheriff fires shot after shot until he hits a pressurized tank which has lodged in the shark's jaws, blowing up the beast and ending the movie.

Grizzly so closely follows the Jaws story that the producers must be embarrased. It starts with a killer bear making a surprising appearance in a Georgia national park where Ursus acrtos horribilis has most likely never lived. Snorting and panting through the forest, Grizzly first mauls two young female campers. Then the movie settles into a routine — sort of like watching the same Red Cross training film 20 times in a row. With considerable gore, the monster moves from murder to murder. There is probably more fake blood in this film than any "wildlife" movie ever made.

The hero — this time the local park ranger — wants the park closed. But the park superintendent, with his eye on a plush Washington job, refuses. As a grand finale, the bear attacks a helicopter, but with a second to spare, the ranger blasts the killer into ashes with a rocket launcher.

The movie was so riddled with inaccuracies and melodramatic fantasy that it amused those familiar with the real grizzly. Unfortunately, most viewers didn't think it was funny.

Each time Grizzly tore up somebody, all those children in the theater cowered, screamed, and hid their eyes. Mauling after mauling, they seemed to build up an intense hate for this terrible beast. And when the hero blew the bear to bits, they let out a cheer resembling the reaction to the home team pulling out the game at the last second. Yes, it worked, just like it did in Jaws. The crowd went home thinking this was the grizzly bear.

Sharks and grizzly bears strike similar notes in human minds. Both are big, fierce-looking, dangerous, unknown, uncommon, and have eaten a few humans. People fear the unknown, a fact cultivated by weak-headed movie makers. For example, the real grizzly definitely didn't fit into this predetermined story, as facts always foul up a good fantasy. Nor would a movie about a 400-pound berry-eater make much money.

How will the viewers of Grizzly react to pleas to save the silvertip? What will they think about re-establishing grizzlies in wild lands where the bear has been exterminated? Will they condone Park Service cut-backs in hiking and camping to leave refuges for grizzlies?

91

Such misinterpretations (not merely movies, but television programs, magazine and newspaper articles, and adult and children books) set sincere efforts to increase or stabilize bear populations back decades. They also intensify the public's lack of sensitivity toward the big bear, whose future depends on people tolerating him — at least in his remaining range and perhaps later in presently unoccupied habitat.

Distortions of bear behavior can, however, go to the other extreme. In another recent movie, *A Man Who Loved Bears,* the producers, Stouffer Productions, Ltd., portray the grizzly as a peaceful and harmless giant, a description which also misses the point. The silvertip may be harmless most of the time, but when man confronts a wild grizzly, the results may be far from peaceful.

Giving people the impression that no danger exists can be as bad as scaring them with fabricated maulings. If misinformed and unprepared hikers converge on grizzly country, confrontations will surely increase. Not only must bears be made wary of people, people must be made wary of bears. Otherwise more frequent encounters will prompt hatred, fear, and intolerance of the grizzly — sentiment which has heavily contributed to the silvertip's threatened status.

Ironically, this is the reverse of what Stouffer Productions intended. *A Man Who Loved Bears* was meant to counteract bitterness toward the grizzly, particularly that produced by *Grizzly.* But if the Stouffers' film indirectly promotes nonchalant attitudes toward the grizzly, it could mean more bloody confrontations which would infuriate ill feelings.

Stouffer Productions hopes to encourage the re-introduction of grizzlies into Colorado. However, the film may have the opposite, long-term impact on public opinion. Future maulings in other states and provinces may turn sentiment further away from bringing the grizzly back to areas like the Colorado Rockies.

Preferably, the public would have a realistic view of the great bear. Since so few wilderness visitors are mauled, statistically the grizzly presents an insignificant threat when compared to other hazards. However, some grizzlies in some situations are in fact dangerous.

Risk is everywhere in today's world. Indeed, considering the remote chance of even seeing a silvertip, grizzly country may be remarkably safe when compared to urban or even partly developed areas. Thus, if the public accepts Old Ephraim for what he is — a potentially dangerous, but majestic wild animal — bear and man can continue to coexist in western North America.

Chapter 5

THE STORY
BEHIND THE STORY

The three major topics of the preceding chapter — the Yellowstone feud, hunting, and maulings — receive much, perhaps too much, attention. Thus, many people — even those specifically interested in the grizzly's plight — haven't heard much, if anything, about the most serious threats to the great bear. So those hoping to save the silvertip often have vague or incorrect ideas on how to go about it, since they rarely know what really threatens the grizzly with extinction. However, after reading this chapter, they will know.

UNTIL THE GONDOLA CAME

The Gallatin Canyon was a pleasant place until the gondola came.

The change began in the late 1960s when a few big corporations[1] acquired 10,000 acres of scenic real estate in the Gallatin Canyon about

---

[1]Big Sky of Montana, Inc. was mainly owned by the Montana Power Company, Burlington Northern, Inc., General Electric, Chrysler Corporation, Northwest Airlines, and Continental Oil (Conoco). After about six years of steady economic deterioration, the original owners sold most of the recreational facilities to Everett Kircher, a Michigan resort owner. However, the original owners retained control of real estate sales.

eight miles north of Yellowstone Park. A year or so later, a newly formed land development firm, Big Sky of Montana, Inc., told local residents what was coming. And it turned out to be more than a gondola.

It was a giant mountain resort with profuse land sales, up to 3,500 condominiums (mostly for second homes), a ski area, commercial facilities, and much more. Big Sky was a new community with far-reaching, long-lasting, and not-immediately-obvious consequences. Most of all, it was a developer's dream, which was destined to become a nightmare for the Gallatin's grizzlies.

In 1967, the canyon was inhabited mostly by ranchers. Ophir School had a capacity of 60 elementary students, but rarely had that many. (There was no high school.) Everybody knew his neighbors. Along the 65 winding miles of U.S. 191, the only highway through the canyon, travelers found a few cafes, cabins, and country stores.

The West Gallatin River, a blue ribbon trout stream, flows out of the park and through the canyon's stunning scenery. Most residents hunted big game to supplement their winter meat larder. "Outside" hunters came to chase elk in the fall, and tourists hurriedly drove through in the summer.

But the Canyon remained remote and unspoiled — until the gondola came, that is.

In 1968, Big Sky arrived in full force. Condominiums appeared along the West Fork of the West Gallatin River. Soon, two new towns — Meadow Village and Mountain Village — began to fill with escapees from megalopolis, all searching for "the good life." The developers built a gondola and several chair lifts up the slopes of Lone Mountain, a majestic peak straddling the divide between the Gallatin and Madison valleys. Later, a golf course, tennis courts, dude ranches, mobile home "campgrounds," sporting goods stores, bars, cafes, swimming pools, an 11-mile highway spur, and a big hotel and convention center rounded out the developers' plans.

Waving a "good planning" banner, Big Sky eagerly plunged forward, and almost everyone applauded its coming. Even ranchers didn't seem adverse to the giant resort or at least they weren't vocal about it. After all, the Big Sky developers *owned* the land, and they could do whatever they wanted with their property.

Thinking along these lines, canyon residents voted down comprehensive planning and zoning. They viewed it as another government infringement on their lives. Besides, landowners thought that planning would jeopardize their property rights, which are dear to most westerners.

After a few years, the real impact of Big Sky began to surface. Placing a large resort in a semi-primitive region kicks off repercussions that seem impossible to stop.

The peaceful and simple life style gave way to gaudy (pink ski boots!), impersonal clamor. Two out of three residents lived in the canyon only seasonally, and recreation-hungry "outsiders" were now flexing their muscles at the ballot box.

With Big Sky under full throttle, spin-off development — bars, cafes, trailer courts, real estate offices, gambling joints, and second home subdivisions — began to line U.S. 191. Traffic increased, renewing interest in a four-lane freeway to replace the curvy two-lane highway. This represents certain disaster for the trout-rich river, as the present highway barely fits within the valley.

The country school became hopelessly overcrowded, and public funds were appropriated for emergency school expenses — as they were for an 11-mile highway spur into Big Sky and an improvement in the Bozeman Airport (60 miles to the north) to accommodate Big Sky traffic. Furthermore, the public will be burdened once more if a four-lane U.S. 191 wins approval. (Remarkably, people everywhere pay for such improvements, even though they primarily benefit private developers and indirectly threaten natural values such as the grizzly bear.)

Big game herds started to go, too, as developers threw up taverns and subdivisions on or adjacent to vital winter ranges — "so the people could see the elk." Recreation, camping, fishing, snowmobiling, etc. increased extensively.

In just a few years, the sleepy Gallatin Valley grew into a "recreation city" with all the makings of a congested, California-type neon-lined, ski resort strip.

As long-time residents started to think back, their hindsight sharpened. They remembered the planning and zoning they had rejected. They remembered the land exchanges between the Forest Service and Burlington Northern, Inc. (a Big Sky stockholder) which had made the resort possible, and which environmentalists had unsuccessfully fought. They remembered how Big Sky promoters had bragged about their "well-planned" resort, one that would be a model for similar developments of the future. And they remembered the lower taxes, the uncrowded schoolhouse, and the silence. A few of them even thought about the big bear, for all this activity didn't set with the wide-ranging grizzly.

The Gallatin still has grizzlies, elk, open space, clean air, and fair fishing.

Grizzly Country

Only in the wildest parts of North America has the grizzly been able to cling to an uncertain existence. Without these large, protected areas, the grizzly may have already disappeared south of the Canadian border. But these "designated" wilderness areas see more and more use from people interested in back country reaction. Thus, the relatively unknown, "undesignated," or de facto wild areas become increasingly important to the silvertip's survival. Here in this unprotected habitat, every summer day sees the wilderness shrink.

Mission Mountains Wilderness. Bob Anderson photo.

Yellowstone National Park. Jerry Manley photo.

Glacier National Park, Montana. Bill Schneider photo.

97

The Bob Marshall Wilderness. Jerry Manley photo.

Grizzly Country
Threatened

A few of the many areas that soon may be without the grizzly. If the grizzly population south of Canada depends on such areas remaining wild and unroaded, the big bear is undoubtedly in big trouble.

The North Fork of the Flathead River, the western boundary of Montana's Glacier National Park. Is this the future site of open pit coal mining operations large enough to remove entire mountains, natural gas pipeline networks and refineries, and sprawling second home subdivisions? Bill Schneider photo.

The serene Sunlight Basin, just east of Yellowstone National Park. Is a massive mining venture planned for this valley without the public even knowing about it? Lynne Bama photo.

The Slough Creek Corridor, just northeast of Yellowstone Park and separating the rugged Beartooth and Absaroka mountain ranges. Will a tourist highway be built through the corridor to bring more people into Yellowstone Park and indirectly promote mining developments in the Beartooth and Absaroka ranges? Bob Anderson photo.

100

The Gallatin Canyon, north of Yellowstone Park. In the early 1970s, the Big Sky resort moved into the canyon and started a seemingly endless procession of indirect or "spin-off" developments — bars, cafes, trailer courts, improved roads, bigger power lines, etc. Will such "progress" drive the grizzly from the Gallatin Canyon? Bill Schneider photo.

Mount Hebgen, a few miles west of Yellowstone Park. Is this grizzly habitat an appropriate place to put Ski Yellowstone, another massive mountain resort like Big Sky? Bill Schneider photo.

The Madison Range, in southwestern Montana, probably the most threatened piece of grizzly country in the lower 48 states. Can plans for logging roads, ski resorts, clear-cuts, power lines, rural subdivision, and tourist highways be beaten back to protect grizzlies in the beautiful Madison Range? Bill Schneider photo.

But the future looks bleak, as development continues without adequate regulations. By the mid-1970s, many of the original residents viewed Big Sky's coming as a calamity.

"Landowners who were really disturbed by Big Sky are moving out," Ronda Sandquist, researcher for the National Science Foundation, observes. "The other landowners are starting to develop the attitude of 'Well, it's here, so I might as well make the most of it.' And they're planning subdivisions."

The foundation[1] estimated the 1995 population of the canyon at 51,183 if growth continues unabated — up about 4,000% from the 1970 population of 1,254.

True, survey lines are invisible on the landscape. But they don't make looking forward pleasant, and the Montana Power Company's plans make the future even dimmer.

In view of the widespread belief that the nation needs to conserve energy, the power company's plans don't make much sense. Unfortunately, what happens to be best for the country doesn't run investor-owned utilities or produce big dividends for stockholders. Money runs private utilities, and more energy consumption means more money and bigger dividends.

In the Gallatin, the scenario went like this:

1. Montana Power Company (MPC) joined the Big Sky Corporation as a principal investor.

2. At least partly due to MPC recommendations, Big Sky became a champion consumer of energy. All-electric second homes, swimming pools, and commercial facilities (all energy-intensive construction), and distance from urban centers contributed to waste.

3. During the environmental assessment of the Big Sky project, the Forest Service (FS), the agency charged with preparing the environmental impact statement, never even used the word "energy." Negative aspects of energy extravagance were ignored.

4. In 1971, MPC ran a small, 50 kilovolt (kv) power line down the canyon along U.S. 191 to energize Big Sky.

5. In 1972, MPC started pushing hard for a coal-fired, electric-generating

[1]In 1970, the National Science Foundation and Montana State University launched a well-funded research project to identify, describe, and assess the environmental impact of the Big Sky development. Since then, the study team — mostly MSU professors — has published two reports entitled "Impacts of Large Recreational Developments Upon Semi-Primitive Environments; The Gallatin Canyon Case Study."

complex in eastern Montana, about 200 miles east of Big Sky. MPC's plans for Colstrip closely resembled the infamous Four Corners Plant near Farmington, New Mexico, perhaps the nation's worst industrial polluter. Part of MPC's pitch for this complex[1] was the rapid energy growth of the Big Sky area — a demand the utility had helped create.

Indeed, there was demand. The 1973 peak load of *only* Meadow and Mountain villages (not including other subdivisions and commercial development in the area) exceeded the 1968 peak load of the entire Gallatin Canyon.

"Conservative estimates compiled by the Montana Power Company Marketing Department indicate a tremendous growth rate of 500% between the years 1973 and 1978 for the Big Sky area," the utility noted. "The projected load for Meadow and Mountain Villages at Big Sky, Montana, of 30,000 kilowatts in 1978 is approximately equivalent to the combined peak loads of Bozeman, Belgrade, Manhattan, and their surrounding rural districts."

"Bozeman, Belgrade, Manhattan, and their surrounding rural districts" housed about 40,000 people in 1974. Before Big Sky, the energy needs of the canyon were meager at best, the area served by one very small rural distribution line. Meadow and Mountain villages didn't exist!

6. In 1974, MPC revealed plans to build a big (161 kv) transmission line to Big Sky. However, the utility didn't want to follow the existing corridor along U.S. 191. Instead, the line-builders hoped to energize Big Sky from the west by stringing wires through some prime grizzly habitat. Originally, MPC suggested extending the big line through Big Sky to the east, violating two more roadless regions supporting grizzlies. However, immediate public protest prompted the utility to backtrack on this part of the plan, at least temporarily.

MPC and Big Sky still pushed for a corridor through the roadless backbone of the Madison Range, however. The "need" for this new line was continued growth at Big Sky. Incredibly, this "need" included the future construction of over 2,000 more condominiums, 28 electrically heated swimming pools, and at least one mountain restaurant.

7. Both the FS and the Montana Department of Natural Resources and

---

[1]The Colstrip generating complex is proposed by Montana Power Company in conjunction with four other northwest utilities — Puget Sound Power and Light Co., Pacific Power and Light Co., Washington Power Co. and Portland General Electric Co.

Conservation have researched the power line proposal.[1] The state resources agency has recommended against routing the line through Madison Range grizzly habitat. Instead, the state would prefer the line to go directly up the canyon. Conversely, the FS seems to prefer stringing the big line through grizzly habitat, although the federal agency hasn't made its final recommendation yet. Since the route requires approval from both agencies, the plan will probably sit until decision-makers can agree on where to put it. Unfortunately, though, planners seem to ignore the vital question: Should there be a big line at all? Regardless of how this abundance of power gets into the canyon, the impact remains the same. Some routes are better than others, but this extra electricity will spawn sprawling subdivisions and other developments — much to the grizzly's detriment.

The hard rule of supply and demand has gone astray. Instead of creating supply to meet demand, MPC creates demand to help justify providing the supply. This is like purposely filling a bathtub until it overflows and then shopping for a bigger bathtub to correct the situation instead of simply turning the tap to maintain the water at a reasonable level.

The "need" for the big line — to accommodate more growth in the Gallatin Canyon — is questionable. But violating a prime wilderness area to do it seems unforgivable.

How will this inverted "planning" affect the grizzly? The line will physically alter many miles of habitat, especially during construction. However, this damage is minor compared to the disguised consequences.

First, an abundance of "cheap and clean" electricity will stimulate growth in the Gallatin Canyon, with far-reaching effects on the grizzly and other wildlife, as it haphazardly encourages more people to come to "Big Sky country." ("Big Sky country" used to be grizzly country.)

Second, the line would leave a convenient corridor through a continuous expanse of wild land, which extends from the Spanish Peaks all the way south through the Taylor-Hilgard area, paving the way for another highway to Big Sky from the west. Not surprisingly, local businessmen are already pushing for a road through the corridor. Just as the power line would

---

[1]The State of Montana — through the Department of Natural Resources and Conservation — must study such proposals under its Utility Siting Act, which a later legislature revised into the Major Facility Siting Act. The Forest Service will have to adhere to at least two major federal laws — the National Environmental Policy Act and the Endangered Species Act — in deciding what to do with the power line. Both the state and federal government must approve the line before it can be built.

encourage growth by providing abundant energy, the road would promote development by supplying easy access. Keeping this corridor closed can more likely do more to slow the destruction of the Gallatin Canyon and, in turn, the area's grizzly population than any other single pending action.

As the secondary effects of Big Sky thrash around the Rocky Mountain West like the tentacles of a hyperactive octopus, another developer hopes to repeat the performance. Ski Yellowstone, Inc. plans to build the Gallatin's second giant mountain resort. But Ski Yellowstone prefers to go a step farther than Big Sky by pushing for a "ski corridor." Apparently, ski resorts make more money if they're part of a chain. Refugees from unsmiling cities like to try several resorts instead of spending their winter vacation at one area. Thus, Ski Yellowstone says the Yellowstone Park area needs a ski corridor.

A Ski Yellowstone brochure says this corridor starts at Bridger Bowl (just northeast of Bozeman, Montana). From there, it heads south into the Gallatin Canyon to Big Sky, continues on to Ski Yellowstone and to Idaho's Grand Targhee resort, and winds up at Wyoming's Jackson Hole. Since the other four resorts are already operating, Ski Yellowstone is, according to the brochure, "the essential link" in the corridor.

Completing ski corridors undoubtedly makes resort investors smile. But it also means a 300-mile chain of congestion through much of America's grizzly country. The consequences of five ski areas magnify when one realizes the resorts would, for the most part, be linked by strings of trailer courts, bars, second homes, and perhaps more ski developments.

Ski Yellowstone resembles Big Sky, but it has fewer bedrooms and less private land to subdivide. Ski Yellowstone, which would go on the shores of Hebgen Lake, just west of Yellowstone Park, has only 1,000 acres of private land. However, the developer wants special permission from the Forest Service to place 10 chair lifts, a mountain-top restaurant, several new roads, and another gondola on 6,932 acres[1] of the Gallatin National Forest — public land. The current master plan (such plans change periodically) calls for 618 condominiums, 313 single-family residences, 15 duplexes, 225 employee housing units, a full-service marina, a golf course, two villages, commercial facilities, a shopping mall, an environmental education center, and enough overnight lodging for 1,000 visitors. (This doesn't include the facilities which will be provided by similar developments sure to spring up on

[1]Reacting to widespread opposition, Ski Yellowstone, Inc. later temporarily reduced this request to 1,880 acres.

106

private land on the periphery of the Ski Yellowstone property.)

Ski Yellowstone is "well planned," just like Big Sky. Developers have everything arranged neatly within the development's boundaries, but they haven't looked past the front gate. Ski Yellowstone paid Montana State University professor Dr. John Montagne and several others to write a three-inch-thick, biophysical analysis of the proposed resort. The report glamorized the project, even going as far as to say "many biophysical aspects" of the development site would be "enhanced."

Again like Big Sky, the developers refuse to address the long-term and uncontrollable aspects of moving in a massive mountain resort. Asked about the negative and unplanned aftermath of resorts like Big Sky, Ski Yellowstone's head planner, Gage Davis, of the Denver-based Beardsley-Davis Associates, Inc., said, "We just can't grapple with that. I just don't know how you deal with this sort of thing."

Sooner or later, however, developers and partial-planners must deal with the total impact of their plans; it is their responsibility. The day has long passed when they can wear binders and work in a vacuum for convenience.

By late 1973, Ski Yellowstone promoters had about everything "greased." They claimed to have promises from the FS that there wouldn't be any problems in securing the necessary permits and that the agency would hurry up the environmental review to get it out of the way. They had drummed up a letter-writing campaign from the State Association of Realtors and from businessmen from West Yellowstone (the nearest town). And they had political support from former President Gerald Ford on down. Montana Governor Thomas L. Judge who strongly backed Ski Yellowstone, said that this was the kind of clean industry Montanans want.

Even with this initial success, the developers had to delay their plans for a year. They had originally hoped to start construction in early 1974. Then, their plans started going sour. Many citizens began seeing Ski Yellowstone for what it really was — an energy-intensive, incompletely planned, economically premature second home subdivision in a remote grizzly bear sanctuary.

The big bear's plight helped urge the Montana Wilderness Association (MWA) to take the lead in the budding battle to block the ski corridor. However, the MWA and its many allies did more than oppose the development. They offered, in their words, "a reasonable alternative." They suggested setting aside the area exclusively for nonmechanized winter recreation — primarily cross-country skiing, snowshoeing, and snow camping. Following FS regulations, the MWA applied for a special use permit to study

107

the feasibility of their alternative, just as Ski Yellowstone had.

Beside protecting natural values and grizzly habitat, the citizens' alternative proposal provided some economic benefits for West Yellowstone, from which most of Ski Yellowstone's support was coming. "We don't have millions of dollars to spend, but we can still benefit the local community and should receive equal consideration from the Forest Service," charged Rick Applegate, the MWA coordinator of the alternative effort.

The MWA efforts obviously caught the FS off guard, because the agency sidestepped for months. (Ski Yellowstone had received its study permit on the same day it applied!) Finally, Gallatin National Forest Supervisor Lewis E. Hawkes, gave the MWA permission to evaluate the proposal. However, he wouldn't let the citizen group study the same public land Ski Yellowstone wanted to develop (Mount Hebgen). Hawkes stated that because he had inadvertently given Ski Yellowstone an "exclusive" permit to study this public land, MWA people were to stay off Mount Hebgen while doing their feasibility study.

Unfortunately, Mount Hebgen has the best cross-country ski terrain in the area. So in short, Hawkes said the MWA could only evaluate the less desirable ski-touring slopes around the Ski Yellowstone site.

At first, the FS refused to consider the MWA proposal as a workable alternative to the multi-million dollar development. But the MWA wouldn't accept this. Calling it "ridiculous," the organization challenged the decision and prepared a preliminary report that included Mount Hebgen. "We are not interested in developing nonmechanized winter recreation *in conjunction* with Ski Yellowstone," Applegate wrote in the preliminary report.

Hawkes still wouldn't consider the MWA proposal a viable option to the potentially destructive resort; instead, he termed it "only a blocking action."

MWA volunteers hoped their "development" (their word) would receive equal consideration with Ski Yellowstone's plans. However, the FS appears to have jokingly passed off this positive, sincere, economically promising proposal as the work of obstructionists.

MWA members, other organizations, and local citizens remembered what had happened with Big Sky. In that case, the FS had also served as chief justifier for the development. Big Sky had needed a series of land exchanges between Burlington Northern and the FS. So, after writing an environmental impact statement on the exchanges, the FS went ahead with them.

The far-reaching ramifications of these land exchanges were never

108

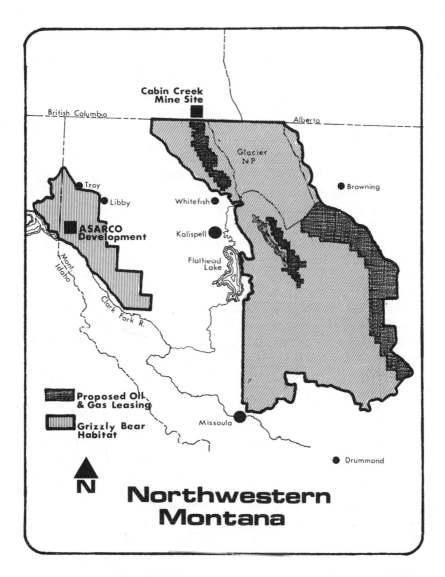

Mapping grizzly habitat is risky business. As surely as the ptarmigan turns white in winter, a grizzly will show up outside the lines drawn on the map. Likewise, there are probably places (roads, small towns, mountain peaks, etc.) within this occupied grizzly habitat where the bear never sets his massive foot. Nonetheless, this map represents the best estimate of remaining grizzly habitat south of Canada. Also indicated are a few of many major developments underway in or planned for grizzly country. It's nearly impossible to list all encroachments into grizzly country, so the map only shows those mentioned in the accompanying text.

investigated. True, the FS came out ahead in number of acres. However, Big Sky foes forcefully pointed out that the public received land which, because of rugged terrain and other factors, would probably *never* be developed, regardless of ownership. Burlington Northern received public land with high development potential, including the site of Mountain Village. After the exchanges, Burlington Northern promptly traded the newly acquired land for stock in Big Sky of Montana, Inc.

Also, the exchanges allowed Burlington Northern to piece together a 30,000-acre block of developable land between Big Sky and Yellowstone Park. Local conservationists suspect this, too, will soon be subdivided.

One MWA member who bitterly recalls how the FS pushed Big Sky into reality charges, "The Forest Service did everything it possibly could to justify Big Sky." And he expects the same with Ski Yellowstone.

Hans Geier, head promoter of Ski Yellowstone, casually admits the FS promised him the corporation would get special permission to develop Mount Hebgen. However, FS officials deny making any such promise. Regardless of what transpired between the FS and Ski Yellowstone, though, the FS appears to be moving steadily along in its attempt to approve this inappropriate development.

Chronologically, the FS review of the Mount Hebgen area proceeded like this:

1. The original land use plan released May, 1974, made a fair attempt to address the grizzly problem. Much of the Mount Hebgen area, including the proposed site of Ski Yellowstone, was classed as "key" grizzly habitat. The plan also noted the national significance of grizzly habitat. About the same time (July 19, 1974), Jerome T. Light, Jr., a biologist working at the Gallatin National Forest, reinforced the Forest Service commitment to the grizzly by recommending in an inter-agency memo that the FS "maintain the continuity of [grizzly] habitat...in an undisturbed state."

2. Then, the Ski Yellowstone project started gathering steam, and the planning process took an about-face. In the Draft Environmental Statement on the Hebgen Planning Unit (released December, 1974), grizzly habitat was largely ignored. The draft statement also suggested a "winter sports complex" that conformed to Ski Yellowstone's plans.

3. In the Final Environmental Statement on the Hebgen Planning Unit (released November, 1975), the FS walked the tightrope on the grizzly situation. The bear had recently been classified as a threatened species, which apparently prompted a few token statements about the grizzly. However, the "key habitat" outlined in the original land use plan became

110

"potential habitat."

4. The Draft Environmental Statement specifically addressing ski development (released September, 1976) strongly recommended the Ski Yellowstone project over the Montana Wilderness Association's nonmechanized recreation area and the nondevelopment alternative. This recommendation was made even though the FS stated in the draft statement that the resort would hurt critical grizzly habitat. In response to this draft statement, the Montana Department of Fish and Game sent in this official comment: "It is our recommendation that the area be treated as very important to grizzlies until shown to be something else. We feel that it is indisputable that if Mount Hebgen and the surrounding area presently has value to grizzlies, [the grizzly] would clearly be adversely affected by the development of Ski Yellowstone and the resulting increased human activity in the area."

5. On May 13, 1977 the FS released the Final Environmental Statement on development of Mount Hebgen. Not surprisingly, the federal agency, in conflict with the Carter Administration promises to promote energy conservation, continued its full support for the energy-extravagant resort. The "key and potential" grizzly habitat mentioned in earlier FS documents was ignored completely. Instead, the FS noted: (1) "There would be no modification of identified grizzly habitat in connection with the ski area development." and (2) "There is no identified grizzly habitat in the area applied for."

The majority of public comment has gone against Ski Yellowstone (over 2,000 people have sent in comments), and the economic feasibility of the resort has grown increasingly suspect. Nonetheless, the developers forge forward, with the FS meeting their demands.[1]

Throughout the environmental review of Ski Yellowstone, citizens and agencies urged the FS to carefully address the grizzly's plight. However, the federal agency continually sidestepped and minimized this all important issue.

In presenting the alternative proposal, MWA President Doris Milner

---

[1]Although the FS approval of Ski Yellowstone in Final Environmental Statement on ski development was the agency's final choice, it's unlikely that the development will proceed for a year or more, as citizens' groups will appeal the decision through administrative and legal channels. Such appeals may succeed in halting the development. A copy of the Final Environmental Statement is available from the Gallatin National Forest, Federal Building, Bozeman, MT 59715.

strongly stated, "The MWA plan would be withdrawn immediately if there was the slightest chance it would affect the grizzly." When Hans Geier was asked if Ski Yellowstone would likewise withdraw its plans if they would harm the grizzly, he refused to answer, calling the question "hypothetical."

Wildlife professionals, on the other hand, consider the development anything but "hypothetical." Although they argue about how seriously Ski Yellowstone will affect the grizzly, biologists agree that the resort means bad news for the big bear. For example, John Cada, game biologist for the Montana Department of Fish and Game, says, "There is no doubt in my mind that the proposed Ski Yellowstone development will adversely affect grizzly habitat."

Cada, who is responsible for wildlife management in the Hebgen Lake area, also notes; "That is key grizzly bear habitat. And grizzlies presently inhabit the area. However, the area could support even more grizzlies unless the wrong kind of land use prevents the population from expanding."

Confirming Montana Department of Fish and Game feelings on Ski Yellowstone, LeRoy Ellig, Cada's supervisor, wrote to the FS, "Our option does not include a ski development on Hebgen Mountain. We must oppose a recreation development in the center of key grizzly bear habitat. It is our feeling that if such a development were allowed on public land, it would clearly be a step backward in any attempt to preserve key grizzly bear habitat."

Ski Yellowstone backers, including West Yellowstone businessmen, worked hard to silence department professionals by going to the governor and to the politically appointed Fish and Game Commission which oversees the department, and even threatening legal action. Although Governor Judge renewed his support for Ski Yellowstone, the Fish and Game Commission resisted political pressure, backing the department view of the development. Later, the commission made its stand official in an October 1, 1975, letter to the Gallatin County Board of Commissioners: "This proposed development and associated ski area, if constructed, will cause adverse and irreparable damage to grizzly bear habitat and will certainly increase conflicts between grizzly bears and people."

Ski Yellowstone's own biophysical analysis, written by Brent Haglund, stated that grizzlies most likely frequent the development site. And grizzlies and grizzly sign have recently been sighted on and very near the site. Yet, the developers persistently refuse to acknowledge any adverse impact on grizzly habitat. "Just because one grizzly bear ran through there five years ago doesn't make it key grizzly habitat" was how their argument went.

112

Biologists also bring out evidence of an expanding grizzly population, thus making potential but underoccupied or unoccupied habitat vital. ("Expanding" doesn't necessarily mean "increasing.") Although researchers won't commit themselves until all the facts are in, there is considerable data to indicate that the closed dump policy in Yellowstone Park caused grizzlies to "spread out" and search for new homes.

Formerly, many (maybe *too many*) bears ranged around the park's interior, feasting on human trash, with this extra food source perhaps holding the bear population above the capacity of the habitat. When the dumps disappeared, bears were forced to depend on natural foods. Since there were probably not enough berries to go around, some bears migrated out of the park in search of secure living. Testifying to this, grizzly sightings have steadily increased in the past few years around Mount Hebgen, according to Ken Greer of the Montana Department of Fish and Game.

The developers tried to counter claims of grizzly habitat damage. They had Brent Haglund revise his original study with an addendum which downplayed Ski Yellowstone's potential impact on the big bear, and they sent their consultant, Don Alford, to urge bear authorities to soften their stand.

The resort's backers knew their development was in serious trouble because it would make life tougher for the threatened grizzly. But the only way they could avoid hurting the big bear was to not build Ski Yellowstone, an option which obviously didn't appeal to them. So they set their heels for the impending debate, standing by their claim that the resort would go on the edge of grizzly habitat, not actually in it.

Even if this were true, the development would still hurt the grizzly, as it would remove a vital buffer zone that now cushions the bear from civilization. With this buffer gone, a slice of grizzly country adjacent to the resort would become the new cushion, and once again, the grizzly would come out with less room to live.

Surprisingly, the FS itself recently emphasized the need for this buffer. Dr. Albert Erickson, a long-standing bear authority, completed a study for the FS[1] which emphasized the importance of this buffer zone. "While this is dependent upon circumstances," Erickson wrote, "I would judge that insofar as possible, an attempt should be made to provide a minimum buffer

[1]Erickson, Albert W., Ph.D., "Grizzly Bear Management in the Seeley Lake Ranger District," Lolo National Forest, June, 1975.

of 2 miles between all areas of prime grizzly habitat and areas of human activity."

At the very least, Ski Yellowstone would go well within this 2-mile buffer zone. But apparently, the Forest Service isn't listening to itself.

It must be stressed again that the physical on-site impact of such development is dwarfed by the secondary effects. Ski Yellowstone developers don't like to discuss these distant uncertainties, mainly because they can't control them. Once the developers have the necessary permits, they remain strangely silent when secondary issues pop up — new roads, bigger power lines, energy shortages, spin-off developments, and increased burden on taxpayers for improvements such as schools, highway maintenance, and airports.

Liz Smith, a leading Montana environmentalist, likens this situation to a large shark moving into new waters followed closely by pilot fish. When a big shark (Big Sky or Ski Yellowstone) moves in, it inevitably brings pilot fish (spin-off developments) to fatten on the scraps the large fish casts off. In addition, consider the following:

• The Hebgen Lake vicinity already has hundreds of second home lots and residences for sale.

• The national trend is moving away from mechanized, energy-intensive recreational opportunities.

• Economists are questioning Ski Yellowstone because the trends on which plans for the development were based are collapsing. (For example, Big Sky and several similar mountain resorts in Colorado can't sell condominiums because of the slumping second-home market.)

• The major fault responsible for the 1959 Yellowstone earthquake passes only one-half mile from Mount Hebgen. The epicenter of the quake was Red Canyon, which is adjacent to the development site.

In spite of these drawbacks, the developers keep pushing for their resort. In doing so, they often assume the role of community savior, insisting the survival of the local economy depends on their development. And their diligence is paying off, as the development appears to be on its way to securing the necessary permit from the Forest Service. In the end, a win for the developers will be a loss for the grizzly. But this doesn't stay their enthusiasm to build Ski Yellowstone.

The step-by-step progress of development of the Gallatin Canyon is presented as an example of how civilization is encroaching on grizzly country and how difficult it is to deny such encroachment. Nationally, people want the last grizzly habitat protected, but if Ski Yellowstone typifies the trend, human encroachment is, at best, difficult to curb — even when the development goes on public land and the public opposes it.

Of course, developers don't want wildlife to waste away or air to become polluted, since a clean environment entices buyers. However, these undesirable effects automatically accompany the desirable — although few developers or buyers of rural condominiums will openly accept this truism. And those who realize it but still opt for these massive resorts imply that developing the last primitive places for mass recreation takes priority over grizzly habitat. In the final analysis, such recreational and residential development may be the most formidable threat to America's vanishing king, the mighty grizzly bear.

As the Gallatin gradually grows, it will gradually lose its most outstanding wild resident, the grizzly. And along with the bear will go many things that made the canyon such a pleasant place — before the gondola came.

THE GALLATIN GOES ON AND ON

The saddest part of the Gallatin Canyon story is that it isn't restricted to this single, scenic valley. It is, in fact, only the beginning — merely a good example of what's happening all across grizzly country. It would take many books to completely cover civilization's encroachment into Old Ephraim's already-limited home.

Names and figures change, but the purpose remains the same — to reap profit for land developers, Realtors, energy companies, stockmen, woolgrowers, loggers, and commercial interests. To some of these profiteers, the grizzly isn't worth much — especially when controversy over preserving the bear's habitat stands in the way of "progress." Worse, federal agencies allow or even encourage this single-minded exploitation of public land. For example, in 1970, the Chief of the Forest Service said his agency should "identify and promote opportunities for community development including new towns and insure that Forest Service programs contribute fully to their growth."[1] In line with this philosophy, the Forest Service had earlier created the town of West Yellowstone by withdrawing land from the national forest for urban development. Later, the same agency made Mountain Village at Big Sky possible with a land exchange.

Likewise, the National Park Service encourages residential development

[1]From a 1970 pamphlet entitled *Framework for the Future.*

115

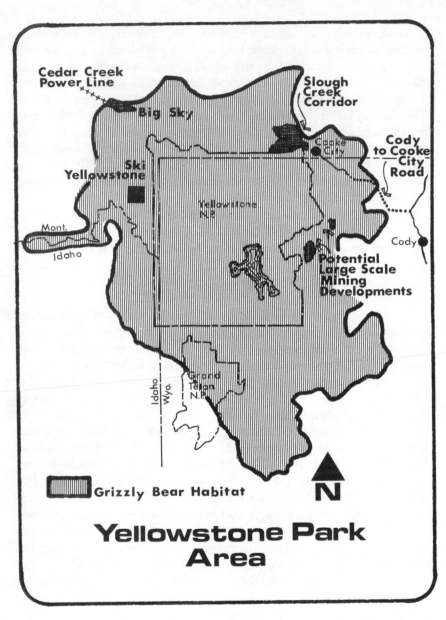

Cedar Creek
Power Line

Big Sky

Slough
Creek
Corridor

Cooke
City

Cody
to Cooke
City
Road

Ski
Yellowstone

Yellowstone
N.P.

Mont.

Idaho

Potential
Large Scale
Mining
Developments

Cody

Idaho
Wyo.

Grand
Teton
N.P.

▓▓▓ Grizzly Bear Habitat

N

Yellowstone Park
Area

Like the map of northwestern Montana on page 109, this map of grizzly habitat in the Yellowstone Park area is merely the best available estimate. And again, only the developments mentioned in the text are indicated.

in grizzly country. A "management objective" listed in the Yellowstone National Park master plan reads, "Every encouragement and assistance should be given to the development of visitor overnight accommodation outside and within an hour's driving distance of the park."

Granted, some public land and most private land will eventually fall into commercial use to keep the economic system running. But the development trend in grizzly country is hardly the answer to economic problems. Resource overuse and unneeded recreational development — especially the high density, mechanized variety — may provide short-term profits for certain businessmen and a few more years of affluent living for an undetermined fraction of the American populace. But regardless of how this kind of development is rationalized, it's at the expense of much of the mighty grizzly's last habitat as well as other worthy parts of the western way of life — uncrowded living, drinkable streams, friendly neighbors, good hunting and fishing, uncluttered vistas, and agricultural life styles — to name a few.

In considering management of the silvertip's remaining retreats, the greatest, overall, long-term good lies in maintaining as much viable grizzly habitat as possible. This is equivalent to maintaining as much of this country's natural integrity as possible for future benefit and study.

But public interest has little influence in grizzly country. Because local residents are few, for the most part (that's why there are still grizzlies!), a big developer or an organized group of profit seekers can snowball an inappropriate development into reality while most of the bear-loving public look the other direction.

Take the Henry's Lake/Island Park region in Idaho just west of Yellowstone Park, for example. As in the Gallatin Canyon, second home development has gone wild. Here, most of the subdividable land lies within the Targhee National Forest, in (or on the fringe of) grizzly habitat. Like the Gallatin, this region attracts mass recreational development and land sales because of its proximity to Yellowstone Park, clean air and water, abundant wildlife, and scenic grandeur. As developers conquer this region, the big bear will slowly fade away — the more development on private land the further into public owned habitat the impact reaches. This gradual moving in on the grizzly has already had its telling signs. In 1971, for example, a seasonal resident shot a grizzly on her front porch as the bear rummaged through the garbage can.

Ski Yellowstone wants its "ski corridor" to cut through this area on its way to the Grand Targhee ski area, 50 miles south of Henry's Lake. This "corridor," coupled with loose control of rural subdivision, will certainly

117

congest the region.

This is unfortunate because at least one important grizzly region, the Centennial Mountains, lies west of U.S. 191. Certainly, the Centennial region has the potential of supporting more grizzlies than it presently does. However, such an increase may never occur if the "ski corridor" cuts off the region from the Yellowstone Park area, creating an isolated, remnant population which is more vulnerable.

GET THE SHEEP OUT

However, recreational subdivision and absence of sound planning aren't the only problems in Idaho grizzly habitat. Here, the FS still allows domestic sheep grazing right up to the Yellowstone Park boundary. Domestic stock also graze grizzly country in Montana and Wyoming. In Idaho, though, the conflict between domestic livestock and grizzlies seems especially intense.

Basically, sheepmen run their flocks at bargain rates on publicly owned summer range, a practice that is not uncommon. In fact, nearly all public land with any grazing potential — except the national parks and a few other areas — is grazed. In Idaho's Targhee National Forest, four ranchers run about 16,300 sheep just west and south of the park.

The conflict comes from a long-established antagonism of the livestock industry toward big predators, and this attitude has carried over into modern times under "The only good grizzly is a dead grizzly" rationale. With some exceptions, Old Ephraim gets blown away every time a sheepherder gets the opportunity.

The Idaho Fish and Game Department has sketchy records of at least 24 grizzlies killed in a scant five years — 1970-74. But the game department officials suspect this estimate is "conservative."

In 1975, Arthur Allen and Carole Jorgensen confirmed this suspicion while studying grizzly bear mortality on the Targhee National Forest. In what appears to be a more comprehensive analysis, they found that 32 grizzlies were killed in the same five-year period.

Predictably, Allen and Jorgensen discovered that the livestock industry

118

accounted for most mortality. "Of the thirty-two bears killed on [the] Targhee National Forest," they wrote in their 1975 report, "twenty-eight died as a result of livestock conflicts." The Interior Department estimates Idaho's total grizzly population at about 100, aptly expressing the significance of the bear/livestock conflict.

For years, Frank DeShon, regional game biologist for the Idaho Fish and Game Department, has been trying, with little success, to do something about this conflict. "The first few years, it was easy to get information," he recalls. "Then, [the sheepmen] found out what we were doing, and they clammed up." ("What we were doing," he adds, was trying to stop the needless killing of the rare grizzly bear.)

"What it boils down to is that they shoot bears wherever they see them — even if they are 10 miles from their sheep," DeShon charges. "Under Idaho law, there isn't much we can do about it."

Grizzlies have been protected in Idaho since 1946, he explains. "But the law also says the sheepherder can protect his property. So we have to be right there to prove otherwise. Enforcement is next to impossible.

"We have had bears which kill sheep," the biologist admits. "There's no denying that. But the effect of the law is to make all bears a target. It seems strange that the Fund for Animals is trying to stop legal hunting in Montana, but this shooting goes on year after year without anything being done about it."

The amount of grizzly predation on livestock has probably been exaggerated. For instance, grizzlies may feed on stock which have died from eating poisonous plants or from other causes. When a stockman sees a silvertip dining on dead stock, he assumes the bear is the culprit and blasts away. Also, the grizzly may be blamed for sheep killed by black bears, coyotes, and other predators.

In their report, Allen and Jorgensen also addressed the controversial question of how extensive the predation actually is. "...It is difficult to accept the consistent high losses attributed only to predators as reported by some permittees [woolgrowers holding FS grazing permits]," they wrote. "Some permittees consistently report losses of eight to ten percent and more, all to predators with no losses in other categories." In their opinion, this inconsistency between permittees and outdated methods[1] of reporting

---

[1]As an example of archaic methods of reporting loses, Jorgensen wrote: "An old time method of assessing losses was to assume all ewes bore two healthy lambs and that any difference between the expected tally for total survival and the actual count represented

losses "...leaves doubt as to the credibility the records may have."

DeShon says sheepmen weren't worried about public reaction to their shooting grizzlies until the Craigheads started making a fuss about the bear becoming extinct. The woolgrowers then saw national sentiment turning to preserving grizzlies at the relatively small expense of eliminating a few grazing allotments. So information on grizzly mortalities suddenly became unobtainable.

E. Lynn Mitchell, district ranger for the Targhee National Forest, acknowledges the problem, calling the killings "well-founded speculation." However, he feels that the attitudes of the permittees are changing from bitter hatred to consideration for the grizzly's plight.

In addition, Mitchell issued an ultimatum to the sheepmen to stop killing grizzlies or lose their grazing privileges. "We laid the law down to the herders," Mitchell explains. "If we even hear a rumor about their killing grizzly bears, we're going to start reducing the permits. There won't be any predator control."

Since removing grazing privileges for public land would, in effect, close down the sheep operations by eliminating the summer range, Mitchell feels the permittees will respond to his order, and thus the grazing can continue. But some wildlife authorities disagree.

As for the possibility of woolgrowers developing new attitudes toward grizzlies, DeShon says, "definitely not." Instead, he feels that sheepmen have simply covered up the bear killings to avoid a national controversy. (In other areas, such undercover conduct has been called "The Three 'S' Club" — shoot, shovel, and shut up.)

DeShon agrees the "no predator control" policy sounds constructive, but he doesn't believe it works because sheepmen still kill grizzlies. Perhaps it has stopped the practice of broadcast predator control — killing or poisoning most predators before taking stock into the area. Certainly, the federal government — through the U.S. Fish and Wildlife Service's Animal Control Section — now rarely kills or poisons bears on public land for the livestock industry, as the agency did for decades. But from what he knows about the situation, DeShon doubts anything keeps sheepmen from killing every bear they see.

Other wildlife professionals in the Targhee region agree, but because of

animals lost to predators. In some cases, this method may still be in practice." In other words, sheep that died from eating poisonous plants, of natural causes, or for any other reason went down as losses to predators.

political ramifications (The livestock industry wields a big club in Idaho.), they were reluctant to talk openly about the bear/livestock problem. For instance, another experienced wildlife professional from the area (who asked not to be named) put his agreement bluntly by saying, "These sheepherders kill every predator they see — and especially grizzly bears."

A later study by David Griffel on the Targhee National Forest verifies this adverse attitude among some permittees. In his 1976 report, Griffel stated: "On the Dog Creek and Squirrel Meadows allotments, the sheepmen insist on control of all bear stemming from the idea that all bear, regardless, are sheep killers. The methods of control practiced are trapping by both a government trapper and the sheep herders and destroying by shooting and killing all free ranging bear seen on the forest. Both of these methods of control were observed being practiced during the course of this year's field season. Free ranging bear were destroyed when possible, at times when sheep were not in the same area as bear. Comments were received from some permittees that bear seen would be destroyed, even after sheep were removed from the allotments and forest. We are not trying to prove that bear do not kill sheep because they do, but this type of action makes all bear vulnerable to the protection efforts of the livestock owner regardless of guilt. This action as well is dangerous to the grizzly who under the Endangered Species Act of 1973 is offered protection by Federal law."

Years of continued frustration in trying to correct this injustice prompt DeShon to declare, "The only solution is transferring these sheep to another area. As long as there are sheep in there, there will be conflicts." He feels the economic impact on ranchers would be minimal if the grazing allotments could gradually be moved to other ranges instead of being immediately terminated.

"I'm tired of being nice," he blasts. "Getting the goddamn sheep out is the only answer. There ought to be one place in Idaho where a grizzly could be safe from sheep grazing. Right now, there isn't. The grizzly needs more help than any other animal on the Targhee."

The Idaho game department has support in this effort. The National Academy of Sciences (NAS), other professional wildlife managers, and most conservation organizations familiar with the grizzly situation have also recommended moving the sheep out. Although the NAS recommended in 1975 that the Forest Service be encouraged to phase out whatever sheep grazing permits may still remain in the Yellowstone ecosystem as rapidly as possible, there has still been no cut back.

"These agencies have been run by the livestock interests for years,"

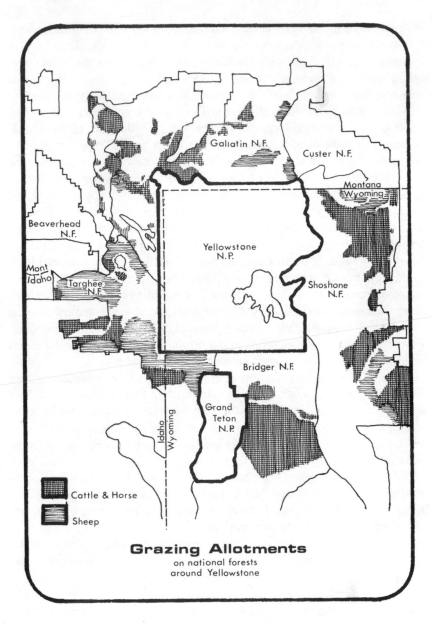

Grazing Allotments
on national forests
around Yellowstone

Galiatin N.F.

Custer N.F.

Montana
Wyoming

Beaverhead
N.F.

Yellowstone
N.P.

Mont
Idaho

Targhee
N.F.

Shoshone
N.F.

Bridger N.F.

Grand
Teton
N.P.

Idaho
Wyoming

Cattle & Horse

Sheep

In spite of repeated protests from the scientific community, conservation groups, and wildlife managers, federal agencies haven't cut back on livestock grazing in grizzly habitat around Yellowstone National Park.

122

DeShon charges. "It's going to take a lot to overcome that. We can't do much unless pressure comes from the national level."

Apparently, a handful of woolgrowers have somehow mustered enough political clout to resist every effort to phase out the grazing permits. So the sheep stay in the Targhee as they do in other public ranges around Yellowstone (see map page 122). Because many local people side with the stockmen, the conflict won't be resolved without a national drive to pressure the federal government into action.

The conflict over grazing permits seems similar to the debate over classifying the grizzly as a threatened species. In the latter case, national pressure for the status countered local opposition to it. So the same sort of national movement may "get the goddamn sheep out."

Although the Targhee sheep problem typifies the conflict occurring whenever domestic livestock graze grizzly country, other areas have similar situations. John Cada, Montana game biologist, also had bad experiences with woolgrowers. In July, 1974, a sheepherder bragged to his barroom buddies that he had just blasted a grizzly. Before long, the Department of Fish and Game caught wind of the story, and asked Cada to check it out.

Cada soon learned the full story. Vern McLain was watering his horses when a bear came out of the timber and headed in the direction of a flock of sheep which was still about a half mile away, Cada recalls. "Even though the sheep were out of sight and had a sheepherder with them, Vern felt the bear would get into them, so he shot him. The first shot struck the grizzly broadside, causing him to turn and charge. The sheepman kept shooting, breaking the bear's hind leg," the biologist notes. "Then, he ran out of shells, so he jumped on his horse and got out of there. Vern and his companions back at the sheepherder's camp decided not to go back and finish off the bear because it was too dangerous." (When the time came for McLean to tell his story to the Forest Service, he changed the facts, saying he had shot the bear in self-defense when it charged right into camp.)

Later, Cada checked Buck Creek, where the incident had occurred, and found bloody beds where the bear had rested temporarily. "Some people saw a grizzly with a dragging hind leg about a month after that," he remembers. "So I suppose the bear could have made it through the winter.

"He's a typical sheepherder," Cada charges. "And that's the typical unhappy ending when you have sheep and grizzlies on the same tract of public land. Montana law says ranchers can dispose of predators that are a threat to their stock. But the way sheepherders think — if it's a bear, it's a threat. This guy figured if he let the bear go, it would get his sheep sooner or later. Even if the bear is in the same valley, it's a threat."

Another hotbed of the sheep vs. grizzly conflict is the Centennial Mountains region, just west of Yellowstone Park on the Idaho/Montana border. Here, the Agricultural Research Service (ARS), an experimenting arm of the U.S. Department of Agriculture (USDA), runs about 3,000 woolies on public land supporting a struggling grizzly population.

"Grizzly bears and wolves are not compatible with sheep productuction," Clarence Hulet, director of the experimental sheep station, angrily reacts when asked about the problem. "What do you think grizzlies eat?

"There are lots of places in the country where there are grizzly bears," Hulet charges, "but this is the only experimental sheep station. The public needs food and fiber. In these times of food shortages and starvation, which do we need more — grizzlies or sheep?"

Local conservationists and wildlife people generally agree with Hulet — grizzlies and sheep aren't compatible. However, they disagree on the solution. Predictably, Hulet and the USDA want the grizzlies to be controlled and the sheep to stay. Conversely, bear supporters want the sheep out.

The Bureau of Land Management (BLM) administered almost all of the Centennial Mountains until 1922, when 15,836 acres were withdrawn from the public domain for "experimental sheep grazing." Today, the BLM administers the land around the station and still maintains some authority over the ARS lands.

It's an unusual arrangement, to say the least. The University of Idaho (the State of Idaho) owns the sheep and receives income and subsidies from them, but the ARS watches the flocks on what apparently is still BLM land. ARS officials won't say exactly how many of the sheep are actually involved in any research. But the sheep station critics believe it's a small fraction of the total.

Nobody knew much about this sheep station until 1974, when the BLM decided to make the Centennial Mountains a primitive area. (A primitive area is the BLM version of a wilderness area on national forest land. The two designations are essentially the same except national forest wilderness has statutory protection, whereas BLM primitive areas are created administratively.)

In a briefing document on the proposed Centennial Mountains Primitive Area, the federal agency made a strong plea to preserve rare wildlife. "The pristine qualities of the area are exemplified by several threatened wildlife species, including Montana grayling, grizzly bear, wolf and native cutthroat trout," the briefing document noted. "These fish and mammals are living in an extremely fragile environment completely at the mercy of man. The slightest adverse effect by management could easily tilt the scales and plunge the threatened species into extinction. It is therefore very important we protect their ever-decreasing undisturbed environment. The Centennial Mountains are a rare and isolated area where we have a second chance to refute the philosophy that 'the only thing history teaches is that history teaches us nothing.' Let us make the Centennial Mountains the exception."

Edward Zaidlicz, Montana director for the BLM, followed this plea up in an inter-department recommendation. "...The most urgent action for the Bureau [of Land Management] and the Department [of the Interior] to take on behalf of endangered species is to designate the Centennial Primitive Area and revoke the Agricultural Research Service withdrawal and thus eliminate domestic sheep grazing. This would provide protection for the wolf and possibly the grizzly bear."

Unfortunately, dedication on the part of Zaidlicz and other BLM officials wasn't enough, as Inter-government politics stymied these sincere efforts on behalf of threatened wildlife.

The BLM wanted the sheep out of the Centennial Primitive Area and went all the way to the top of the Interior Department (BLM's parent agency) requesting the revocation of the ARS withdrawal. But the ARS also went all the way to the head desk in the USDA, prompting a high-level bureaucratic shoot-out between Interior and Agriculture. Unfortunately for the grizzly, Interior backed off.

The BLM even suggested allowing sheep grazing to continue within the primitive area, if the ARS withdrawal was revoked. But the sheep people wouldn't agree.

Battered from its bureaucratic battle, the BLM retreated and classified the land *around* the withdrawal as a primitive area, even though they had previously stated that the ARS lands were essential to the establishment of the primitive area. The agency had also termed the ARS lands the "guts" of the total proposal.

So the sheep stay, and the conflict over grizzlies goes on unabated. Although the BLM received considerable support during its drive to help the grizzly, apparently it wasn't enough to change long-established use of this public land, regardless of how the grazing affected the threatened grizzly.

HOT WATER WASTELAND?

But sheep/grizzly problems are minor compared to the possibility of full development of the area's geothermal resources.

Geothermal developers tap the earth's hot water and make the resulting steam turn turbines, thus creating electricity. And hot water speculators have come to grizzly country in a big way. Dick Heniger, spokesman for the Targhee National Forest, says speculators have already filed for leases on "about a half-million acres." Most of the leasing is in the Island Park district, just west of the park.

Any geothermal development in the Targhee will be, according to George Neilson from the Denver BLM office, "very similar to the Geysers Basin in California." This could mean dozens of power plants (about 120 megawatts each), transmission lines, pipelines, new roads, hundreds of wells, and other associated facilities and activity. Neilson said the hot steam can only be transported for a half-mile, requiring many power plants. Each plant pulls steam from about 16 wells, guaranteeing that most of the activity will be on-site. With coal, gas, and oil development, a refinery or power plant can often be located away from a fragile area, but not with hot water projects.

Sarah Johnson, FS biologist at the Targhee, sums up the probable impact of geothermal leasing as "a complete disaster for the grizzly" if full development proceeds.

John Lloyd, of the U.S. Fish and Wildlife Service in Billings, Montana, echoes Johnson's concern. "It would be a nightmare," he claims. "The whole country would be laced with roads, power lines, pipelines, and power plants. We wouldn't have anything left."

Although the impact of geothermal leasing in grizzly country[1] could be disastrous, it's unlikely it will proceed full steam until the 1980s. The BLM, which manages geothermal exploration and development on public land, won't complete a full environmental impact statement on the leasing until at least 1978, according to Lloyd.

---

[1]Developers and/or speculators have also filed for leases on (1) 30,040 acres in Wyoming, just south of Yellowstone Park, (2) 9,680 acres in Wyoming's Lincoln County on the Idaho/Wyoming border, (3) 12,040 acres around Chico Hot Springs, just north of Yellowstone Park, in Montana, (4) 15,080 acres around Gardiner almost on the park's north boundary in Montana, and (5) 2,900 acres near West Yellowstone on the park's west boundary. Montana and Wyoming leases total about 69,740 acres, magnifying the potential impact of the Idaho geothermal activity.

With energy shortages intensifying, the area's ability to support grizzly bears probably won't mean much when the time for decision comes. If the present trend toward exploitation of public land for energy resources prevails, the federal government will want that hot water out of the ground fast. And the big bear will just have to go somewhere else — if there is such a place for Old Ephraim.

PROGRESS?

After detailing so many serious conflicts over grizzly habitat in Idaho and Montana, it would be a welcome change to say Wyoming didn't have such problems. But the Cowboy State also seems bent on squeezing out the big bear.

Perhaps the most severe current impact on Wyoming's grizzlies comes from the new Clarks Fork road, a 63-mile tourist highway through or on the fringe of the state's best grizzly habitat. The new road, which is now under construction, runs from Cody, Wyoming, northwest and joins U.S. 212 on the Montana/Wyoming border. From there, travelers follow U.S. 212 through Cooke City on their way into Yellowstone Park.

U.S. 212 from Billings, Montana, to the park crosses lofty (10,947 feet) Beartooth Pass and can't be kept open during winter, thus isolating the Cooke City region around the northeastern entrance to the park during winter. Until the Clarks Fork road is completed, winter recreationists can only get to Cooke City by driving 52 slippery miles from Gardiner, Montana, at the north entrance to the park.

"Progress-minded" residents of Cooke City and Cody saw the all-weather road between the two tourist towns as a great wallet fattener. They pushed hard for it, and they won. State and federal officials have approved the road, including a special use permit from the Forest Service to cross the Shoshone National Forest.

Larry Roop, of the Wyoming Game and Fish Department, doesn't enjoy thinking about what will happen to the big bear when road builders open this scenic region for land developers and mobile tourists. "That highway and the recreational development associated with it will have as much impact as Ski Yellowstone," Roop predicts. "We'll have a 1,000% increase in use of this area. In fact, the whole area will change immensely."

Developers will subdivide the private land, and commercial shops will dot the roadway to siphon off the tourist dollar. More and more people will come, and the bear will go. It's an old story.

127

Progress Comes To Grizzly Country

New tourist roads such as this one under construction between Cody, Wyoming and Cooke City, Montana bring more people into grizzly country. The secondary impact of such "improvements" — rural subdivision, bars, cafes, resorts, hamburger stands, tourist traps, etc. — have a severe and long-lasting impact on the great bear. Once such a road has been built, there's no stopping the secondary or "spin-off" development. Bill Schneider photos.

The present gravel road between Cody and Cooke City where it enters the Shoshone National Forest. Farther along....

...motorists encounter highway contractors busy "improving" this primitive road into....

...this — a modern, all-weather, 55-mile-per-hour tourist thoroughfare, U.S. 212 just east of Cooke City. Soon the entire trip between the two tourist towns will be on such a road.

The Wyoming Highway Department mentioned this secondary development in the five-pound Final Environmental Impact Statement the agency wrote on the road — "It is impossible to assess the probable land development impacts...."

The environmental statement claimed the purpose of the new road was "to provide a facility that will fulfill functional needs of this segment of road" — whatever that is. According to highway officials, the road will also boost winter tourism and "tensions and frustrations now experienced in driving a narrow, unpaved, mountain roadway will be relieved, providing the opportunity to enjoy the scenic quality of the corridor."

In its incredibly insensitive environmental statement, the Wyoming Highway Department also pooh-poohs any negative impact on grizzlies and other wildlife the road may have: "Compared to the total habitat available to this resource, the land utilized for the roadway is insignificant.

"In fact, revegetation of disturbed areas results in a more lush growth than exists initially," the environmental assessment continues. "No impact is anticipated on the bear population due to highway construction. An occasional grizzly bear might become a nuisance animal, although this would be a rare event."

This assessment doesn't conform to the opinions of wildlife professionals, who see the road drastically affecting grizzlies. Like Idaho and Montana, Wyoming is putting new emphasis on grizzly research, and Roop, who is responsible for Wyoming's grizzly research, is finding the area more important to the silvertip than originally envisioned. In 1975, for example, he live-trapped a grizzly within one-half mile of the formerly unimproved dirt road winding through the region. The researcher attached a radio transmitter to the grizzly, and subsequent signals showed the silvertip crossed the road in his daily wandering.

This grizzly may be the last one Roop traps near this road, though, as contractors are busy improving it into another year-round entrance to Yellowstone Park. The park is already struggling to handle the visitors it attracts, but profit-minded locals are nonetheless glad to have another 55-mile-per-hour highway through grizzly country to further promote an already out-of-hand tourist business.

New highways must be en vogue, as Cooke City promoters have now joined with their counterparts in Big Timber, Montana, in heralding yet another tourist road through grizzly country. On its way to Big Timber, the proposed road would head north from Cooke City and cut through the Slough Creek Corridor which is presently an umbilical link between two wild

130

lands — the Absaroka and Beartooth mountains. Like the Clarks Fork road, a highway between Cooke City and Big Timber would further restrict the big bear's habitat.

The FS claims jurisdiction to a century-old right-of-way through this corrdior. Commendably, the agency has, for once, sided with the grizzly by closing the corridor and recommending that it be included in the Beartooth Wilderness proposal.

However, Montana county commissioners from Park and Sweetgrass counties also want the corridor. They have, in fact, initiated litigation to force the FS to give up the right-of-way. If the counties gain control over the right-of-way, a road could be punched through the corridor.

If constructed, the highway will cut grizzlies off from the rugged Beartooth Mountains. Currently, bears can pass from Yellowstone Park through the Slough Creek area and into the Beartooths. But this movement might end, if the road goes in.

The new road would promote the same type of tourist-trap development lining the other entrances to the park, but more serious, an all-weather road would encourage efforts to extract minerals. One reason for so little mining activity in the highly mineralized Beartooth region has been poor access. But after a new highway is built at public expense, large mining ventures could suddenly be economically attractive.

Eventual development would parallel that of Wyoming, where the Clarks Fork highway passes the entrance to one of the West's most beautiful valleys, Sunlight Basin, which Roop calls "the heart of Wyoming's grizzly country." Unfortunately, this same valley is the site of a future mining development. Only two or three miles from Yellowstone Park, American Metals Climax (AMAX) and other large mining companies, are carefully evaluating mineral deposits in the Sunlight Basin.

A veil of secrecy always surrounds such mining proposals because mining companies hope to avoid corporate competition and pressure from concerned citizens. Therefore, there are few facts on the Sunlight mining proposal available to the public. But apparently, there will soon be open pit copper mining in the Sunlight Basin, which is part of the Shoshone National Forest. Because of archaic mining laws, FS officials, who seem concerned about the project, essentially sit with tied hands.

Even though mining activity is on national forest lands, the public has little to say about it, as mining companies have full rein over the public domain. The FS can only pester a company about details. If a company decides to mine, it mines.

131

At this early date, it's nearly impossible to assess the long-term impact of developing the Sunlight Basin. But it's a cinch that the grizzly won't benefit.

Even worse, the Sunlight project may be repeated in Needle Creek, 40 miles to the south, within the officially designated South Absaroka Wilderness[1] and close to Yellowstone Park. Again, mining companies won't release details, and the uninformed public remains helpless.

More is known about the massive mining project of American Smelting and Refining Co. (ASARCO) underway in the Scotchman's Peak area near Canada on the Idaho/Montana border. But again, the public has been able to do little to prevent or properly regulate ASARCO's Troy Project — even though hard-working citizens' group, Northwest Citizen for Wilderness, has been trying for years. Such mining projects — with their associated residential development, roads, and intensified human use — are completely incompatable with grizzly bears regardless of what industry spokesmen claim or of what "mitigation measures" are approved.

The Scotchman's Peak area lies just west of the Cabinet Mountains Wilderness and still has a few grizzlies. Biologists haven't estimated the population, but most claim it's small and struggling. With ASARCO's Troy Project underway in the Scotchman's Peak area, the silvertip's struggle for survival in the remote region has taken another turn — perhaps the last — for the worse.

NORTH FORK NONSENSE

How much will Americans accept to ride elevators up two floors, live at 72 degrees, make (and throw away) aluminum beer cans, and drive to work alone while bicycles gather dust in the garage? How far will they go for bigger bathtubs, snowmobiles, second homes, tourist roads, and four-wheel-drive Winnebagos? Will they sacrifice the last grizzly country for these conveniences? The residents of northwestern Montana face these questions, as they view the future destruction of the North Fork of the Flathead River and surrounding wilderness.

The North Fork forms the west boundary of Glacier Park. Although a winding, half-dirt/half-asphalt road follows the river on both sides, it's still 30-60 miles to the nearest movie theater. Wildlife abounds, and mostly native game fish inhabit the river. The scenery is outstanding, with spectacular peaks highlighting all horizons. With the exception of some

[1]The South Absaroka Wilderness has been included in the proposed Washakie Wilderness.

logging and residential development on the western side of the river and the primitive roads, the entire watershed remains remote and unspoiled. In fact, many recreationists still drink from the North Fork — something one can't say about many major rivers.

In early 1974, some alarming rumors began sifting down from British Columbia, where the headwaters of the river lie. Something big was brewing, and in September 1974, the story broke.

Rio Algom Mines, Ltd.[1] announced its plans to mine coal only eight miles north of the border, along Cabin Creek, a major tributary of the North Fork. This is the region Andy Russell adored and described in detail when defining *Grizzly Country,* the title of his excellent book.

The magnitude of Rio Algom's plans stagger the imagination. Briefly, they blueprint the following:

- The *removal* of two mountains.
- The construction of a large processing plant to clean the coal and sort out impurities before shipment to Japanese steel mills.
- The construction of a 60-mile rail spur to get the coal out.
- The location of a new town on the shores of the North Fork. In 1975, one could count the year-round residents of this remote region on one hand. By 1980, over 6,000 could reside there.
- The construction of a 40-megawatt power plant to energize the mine, processing plant, and town.

In addition to these specific projects, local people suspect more destruction, such as:

- The opening of more mines. Rio Algom controls Crown land (Canadian public land) leases on a large area on both sides of the North Fork, down to the Montana border and adjacent to Glacier Park.
- The building of a new road east from the proposed mine. This way, it would be only 18 miles to civilization, whereas both Columbia Falls, Montana, and Fernie, British Columbia are about 60 miles. Pressure from the mining community may gain approval for this road. However, rugged terrain (over the Continental Divide) and heavy snowfall may make maintenance and construction costs prohibitive.

---

[1]Rio Algom Mines, Ltd. is part of one of the United Kingdom's largest industrial conglomerates, Rio Tinto Zinc, Ltd. Rio Algom has, in turn, created a subsidary, Sage Creek Coal Co., to mine the Cabin Creek region.

• A highway to the mine from the north, which the business community will want to continue south across the border, paving the way from Fernie to Columbia Falls. The bumpy, dusty road has, to date, deterred rapid rural subdivision growth along the west side of the river, but with an improved road, developers could really begin to move the second home plots.

• The building of a power line into the North Fork region. Like the present road, the absence of electricity has slowed development, but with the improved road, power line, and commercial facilities, there would be no stopping it.

Like all drainages capable of sustaining a viable grizzly population, the North Fork has escaped civilization's advance. But if Rio Algom has its way, "progress" will come to this remote region in a big way.

"The conflict between industrial development and wildlife management is rampant in many parts of grizzly range," Andy Russell recently remarked, "Strip mining is absolutely destructive to grizzly habitat, apart from its detrimental effects to all other kinds of wildlife and fish. When the grizzly goes in such areas, it is gone for good.

"One of the better grizzly habitats left in the East Kootenay region of British Columbia is in the Flathead River drainage south of Fernie," Russell continues. "But if present plans for strip or open-pit mining are allowed, this grizzly population will be wiped out — to say nothing of other wildlife and wrecking of a magnificent piece of wild country."

The international boundary splitting the North Fork drainage complicates citizen efforts to control the Cabin Creek development. Although some strides have been made, hardened veterans of such confrontations believe the B.C. government will soon approve the mining permit.

Francis Singer, a biologist doing research in the North Fork area, believes the increased himan use produced by the Cabin Creek mine could be taps for both wolves[1] and grizzlies in the area. His research indicates the river floodplain and valley floor (much of which is privately owned) are vital to the grizzly. He attributes this importance to the fact that warmer weather at

---

[1] In 1975, Singer verified the presence of a remnant population of northern Rocky Mountain wolves (Canis lupis irremotus) in the North Fork, thus countering claims that the subspecies was extinct. This is the only known wild breeding population of irremotus in the world and the only verified wolf population in the Rockies south of Canada. Singer suspects the remnant population might be springing back after the use of 1080 and other predator poisons was suspended in the area. But his optimism quickly disappears when Cabin Creek mining plans enter the conversation.

134

lower elevations melts snow early, allowing the lowlands to green up with succulent plants relished by grizzlies.

The Montana Department of Fish and Game also worries about extensive development of the bottom land. To date, over one-eighth of the private land along the river has already been plotted. Some of it has been sold; some has been inhabited, but most of it awaits buyers. The department feels development in the river bottom could become a barrier, or at the least "a deterrent," for grizzlies wishing to leave Glacier Park or to use the floodplain. And these threats grow more serious with additional energy developments — this time, south of the border.

Those who cherish the North Fork were still in shock over Rio Algom's plans when the gas company came. In early 1975, Texas Pacific Oil Co., owned by the Seagram Co, Ltd., applied for oil and gas exploration leases on 236,000 acres of grizzly country along the North and South forks of the Flathead.

Texas Pacific's plans match or surpass Rio Algom's in size and scope. And when one considers the proposals together, including the impact of secondary developments — summer homes, logging, and increasing recreational use — the future of the Flathead grizzly looks dismal indeed.

Don Irvine, spokesman for Texas Pacific, puts his company's chances of finding an economically feasible gas deposit at "nine out of ten," but he doesn't feel the likelihood of finding oil is encouraging. Irvine briefly outlines a probable gas development that would include a pipeline system, new roads, heavy truck traffic, at least one refinery-like plant to remove impurities such as sulfur from the gas, and more intense human use of the region. He also says the gas plant should "go in the center of the gas field," which in this case is the middle of the North Fork and/or South Fork regions — in the middle of some of America's best grizzly habitat.

Since the leases cover national forest land primarily, Flathead National Forest officials wrote a lengthy Environmental Impact Statement (EIS) on the proposal.[1] Commendably, the FS removed some of the more fragile areas (big game winter range and roadless lands) from possible development. But the federal agency still recommended going ahead on

---

[1]Since the FS is responsible for the surface values and occupancy of these lands, this agency was charged with preparing the environmental assessment. However, under the Mineral Leasing Act of 1920, the Bureau of Land Management must make the final decision on the leases. In short, the BLM could deviate from FS recommendations. Added complications come from the fact that the U.S. Geological Survey regulates the development after it begins.

135

165,781 acres of leases.[1]

The FS environmental assessment admitted adverse impact on threatened and endangered wildlife, but in the next breath, recommended going ahead regardless. In addition to the threatened grizzly, two endangered species — the peregrine falcon and wolf — stand to lose another round in their battle to survive.

Perhaps the most obvious deficiency in the EIS was its failure to adequately address the development issue. Unless one reads it carefully, he could leave with the impression these were *exploration* leases only. "However, when you grant privilege to explore," Bob Gibson from the Flathead National Forest notes, "you grant privilege to develop."

Unfortunately, once permission to explore public lands for oil and gas has been granted, development can proceed without the public having the option to deny it. Exploration would leave a small mark on the land, but distant ramifications of development would be catastrophic. One could liken this to granting a permit for a freeway on the basis of minimal environmental effects of the road survey line or to giving a drilling crew testing for coal deposits automatic permission to open a strip mine or build a coal-fired generating complex, if they find coal, because the impact of the drilling was minimal.

Fortunately, Flathead residents complained so vehemently about the scarcity of information on development of the leases that they temporarily thwarted Texas Pacific's applications. Even though local Forest Service officials had approved most of the leases, administrators higher in the agency couldn't agree. Under administrative appeals and threats of legal action by the Flathead Coalition,[2] Regional Forester Robert Torheim ordered Flathead National Forest Supervisor Ed Corpe to rework the EIS which granted the leases. Specifically, Torheim wanted Corpe to add information on the potential impact of *developing* the leases.

[1]Because of almost total opposition to the leasing (only 1% favored any leasing), the FS later decided to defer consideration on 73,000 acres of the 165,781 acres the agency had earlier recommended for approval. These lands will be "held in suspense" until critical habitat for the grizzly bear and northern Rocky Mountain wolf is officially designated. Then, if there is no conflict with critical habitat, the leases will probably be approved, emphasizing the importance of critical habitat designation. (Chapter 6 has a detailed discussion of this subject.) Critical habitat aside, the FS recommended going ahead with about 91,000 acres of oil and gas development along the North and South forks of the Flathead River, most of which is important habitat for the threatened grizzly.

[2]The Flathead Coalition is a citizens' organization that draws from all aspects of the community, including the Chamber of Commerce and the Sierra Club.

The vast majority of the Flathead community opposed granting oil and gas leases on public land. Yet, the Forest Service approved them anyway. Apparently only time consuming and costly administrative appeals and litigation can make this public agency respond to public desires, and thus stall the destruction of grizzly habitat.

Unlike many controversies involving commercial development of federally owned grizzly country, the local community sided with the big bear on the Flathead leasing issue. During the public involvement part of the environmental review, at least 95% of the comments opposed any leasing. Apparently, this type of response still ranks as a voice in the wilderness to Washington D.C. bureaucracies, as the federal government approved the leases.

However, when the State of Montana's turn came to evaluate similar applications from Texas Pacific on 7,780 acres of state land in the North Fork region, the outcome was reversed. As with federal leases, the state land leases were met by strong protest. On the state level, however, the opposition to the leasing translated into a sizeable share of the voting populace, so the State Board of Land Commissioners, composed of Montana's five top elected officials, promptly and unanimously denied the leases.

While commenting on the state leases, conservationists made a convincing argument by connecting the lease applications with the Cabin Creek proposal. The U.S. Department of State and the Canadian government were involved in delicate negotiations concerning Cabin Creek, and Flathead residents hoped an agreement between the two nations would prevent destruction of the North Fork. Thus, the argument went, how could the U.S. approve a development sure to damage the North Fork south of the border and then ask Canada to prevent environmental havoc north of the border? Those fighting for the North Fork insisted both federal and state leases must be refused to show Canada that the U.S. was sincere in preserving the North Fork drainage.

Congressman Max Baucus (D-Montana) entered the North Fork controversy and agreed with the conservationist's connection between the two developments. Baucus worked through congressional channels to chop federal funds destined to implement the leasing and was able to win Congress' approval for placing the North Fork and the two other forks of the Flathead River under the protection of the U.S. Wild and Scenic Rivers Act of 1968. Even though the FS has previously proposed naming the three forks of the Flathead as wild and scenic, the federal agency opposed its own

137

proposal during congressional deliberations.

Now that the North Fork has been designated as a wild and scenic river, it will be more difficult — and more sensitive politically — for the U.S. to condone fossil fuel development in the area or for Canada to approve the Cabin Creek development. But still, no action to date actually prevents either proposal, and indications point to both governments' deciding in favor of development and thus against the grizzly.

Unfortunately, the oil and gas leasing frenzy didn't end with Texas Pacific's applications. Energy companies like the chances of finding oil and gas under the mountain wilderness and the result has been pending lease applications for millions of acres of public land in the Rocky Mountain West. Montana alone has over 2 million acres of pending public land leases, much of which is grizzly habitat.

Currently, the federal government is evaluating these applications. So only time will tell if the grizzly will get the back seat, as the bear did in the Flathead National Forest's analysis of Texas Pacific's applications.

Someday, dwindling natural resources and energy supplies will force people to stand up and say, "No more. It's time to change to a national policy dictating conservation, long-range planning, and alternative living." For the grizzly, the question is — will this renaissance come before it's too late? If the FS's handling of oil and gas leasing in the Flathead is any indication, the answer is no. Too many Americans appear willing to change life styles only when they're forced to, which in this case, is when resources are depleted and when natural legacies like the wild grizzly bear are merely memories.

SAWLOGS OR SILVERTIPS?

In the North Fork, and throughout grizzly country, loggers cut deeper and deeper into the last roadless areas. The logging roads seem to "creep in," extended and improved year by year, until gradually an entire drainage becomes roaded. Every summer day sees the wilderness shrink.

Energy development, subdivisions, tourist roads, and mountain resorts leave permanent marks. But logging can be temporary. Although the data isn't conclusive, bear authorities such as Drs. John Craighead, Albert Erickson, Charles Jonkel, and W. Leslie Pengelly agree that timber cutting can have neutral or beneficial results. Unfortunately, the present mentality among timbermen rarely allows a positive result — unless it's achieved accidentally.

138

In planning timber sales, some forest supervisors put the grizzly first, but others give sawlogs priority. The Gallatin National Forest, for example, is going ahead with several timber sales in virgin grizzly country. In Cedar-Bassett Creek, just north of Yellowstone Park, FS plans to log were temporarily beaten back by concerned citizens. However, other timber sales are going ahead in grizzly habitat, with those responsible seemingly oblivious to any negative effect on the threatened bear.

The worst part of logging is road construction. Although bears move out during the actual cutting, they will return unless vehicle use continues on the logging roads. However, if the roads are closed or destroyed after lumbering operations, timber cutting may have a neutral impact on grizzlies.

But in many cases, foresters give lip service to road closures either by closing only the small spur roads, not the main access road, or by failing to close a road *completely*. Inadequate closures that don't totally block off a road allow dirt bikes, four-wheelers, and other off-road vehicles to freely use the road.

A possible beneficial effect of logging can come from removal of the thick forest canopy. This removal allows berry bushes and other plants used by grizzlies to prosper in an area where such vegetation might otherwise occur infrequently.

Wildlife researchers have proved this positive result for big game animals such as elk and deer. When the forest has been opened, it can become good big game range, especially if it's at the proper elevation. Since grizzlies commonly feed on vegetation growing in these open areas, bear students acknowledge the same outcome is possible.

FIRE — A BEAR'S BEST FRIEND?

Forest fires can also create the same situation as logging — opening the forest and encouraging growth of low-growing, succulent, and woody plants. However, forest fires have been strenuously controlled. "Hit 'em hard and keep 'em small" has been the forester's creed for decades. This philosophy has reduced big game herds by allowing conifers to close in on open areas, lowering the quality of the habitat. And fire control may have had the same adverse effect on the grizzly.

For example, overzealous fire control may be one reason the vast Selway/Bitterroot Wilderness on the Idaho/Montana border lost its grizzlies. This may not have been the *only* reason, but it could have been a contributing factor to the bear's disappearance from this remote region.

Fire policy is changing, however. The "all fires are bad" philosophy, actively promoted by Smokey Bear, is slowly caving away to a completely new science — fire ecology. Old school foresters resent this new philosophy, but new blood in the forestry ranks is slowly and carefully studying the real consequences of forest fires and allowing a few research fires to burn in wild areas such as the Selway/Bitterroot Wilderness and Yellowstone Park. This practice will undoubtedly become more common in back country areas, which is most likely good news for the wilderness king.

Wouldn't it be ironical if one of the grizzly's biggest problems turned out to be another bear — Smokey Bear? Could Smokey, with his slick Madison Avenue propaganda, be inadvertently keeping grizzly bear numbers low by encouraging less productive habitat?

SLIPPERY BILL TELLS ALL

Undoubtedly, logging, livestock grazing, mining, recreational sub-dividing, road, resort and power line building, gas, coal and geothermal development and fire control are rapidly paring away the grizzly's last enclaves. But the *total* impact can only be put in proper perspective by adding *all* these destructive forces together and then throwing in hundreds of smaller intrusions — more trails, increased interest in wilderness hiking, off-road vehicle travel, wilderness cabins, and small subdivisions. The *combination* of all these negative influences appropriately describes the big bear's dilemma — *the story behind the story*.

Any single force considered separately belittles the impact. This is the game of developers, who claim a development is "small" or "only one" or "not nearly as bad as...." Thus, the consequences are "minimal," they insist.

The Slippery Bill Subdivision on the southern edge of Glacier Park provides an excellent case in point. It's relatively small (143 acres), and most of the land around it hasn't been developed yet.

The Department of Fish and Game and Dr. Charles Jonkel publicly warned that the Slippery Bill Subdivision would harm grizzly habitat and produce "problem bears." However, the developers, represented by G. George Ostrom of Kalispell, Montana, were unconvinced and persisted in winning approval for and selling lots in Slippery Bill Subdivision.

Predictably, Ostrom stormed into the local game department office one July day complaining about a grizzly "tearing things up" on the subdivision site. This was *before* the development had received approval, which almost

140

guarantees future confrontations.

Game wardens live-trapped the bear and moved him to an area free of subdivision, but the wardens had solved nothing. They had — on the subdividers' request — merely treated the symptoms while ignoring the disease.

Ostrom and his fellow developers certainly didn't help the grizzly's chance of survival, but they did create a community conversation piece, the Giefer Creek grizzly, the bear trapped in the Slippery Bill Subdivision along Giefer Creek.

Louie Kis, warden captain for the Montana Department of Fish and Game, feels this "problem bear" was created when the work crews at Slippery Bill left garbage unattended. The Giefer Creek grizzly then became accustomed to human food, and "he didn't forget," according to Kis, who is responsible for trapping such "problem bears" in that area.

The Giefer Creek grizzly returned to the Slippery Bill Subdivision the next summer (1976) and started breaking into cabins and raising general havoc. The wardens live-trapped the bear *again,* but this time they moved him a great distance — to the North Fork drainage. But the trap-wise bear, which the wardens were now unable to catch, kept breaking into cabins — as many as 40 or 50 of them.

After about two months of newsworthy break-ins, the Giefer Creek grizzly suddenly and strangely disappeared. Rumor had it that some North Fork resident became fed up with the troublemaker and shot him, thus becoming a member of the Three "S" Club. Another popular theory held that a government predator control agent had poisoned the famous bear. But neither theory was supported with hard evidence. And the following spring (1977), both theories were disproved when a hunter legally shot the Giefer Creek grizzly just north of the Canadian border in British Columbia.

As the Slippery Bill Subdivision blossoms into a crowded wilderness community, the seasonal residents will have other "nuisance bears." They will call the wardens in to "take care of them." After awhile, they will see fewer and fewer grizzlies. Perhaps they will worry about the species. Or perhaps they will sit in their second home in the Slippery Bill Subdivision and castigate some agency for mismanaging the grizzly and driving him to extinction, while ignoring their own significant role in the bear's disappearance. And the developers may make some virtuous statement about their concern for the environment on their way to another recreational subdivision in grizzly habitat.

Developments like the Slippery Bill Subdivision only typify the trend —

141

the *story behind the story,* a gradual gnawing away of the grizzly's last domain. Sometimes, this subtle process is hard to comprehend, as people usually have rationalizations justifying their actions while retaining their desire to help the grizzly and environmental quality, in general. But when people like those who bought or sold land in Slippery Bill Subdivision, stock in Ski Yellowstone, condominiums at Big Sky, or wilderness cabins finally wake up, they *will* understand that they have indeed contributed to the grizzly's absence with their wasteful life styles and poor investments. Likewise, those who sit apathetically by and don't protest encroachments into grizzly country or extravagent uses of energy supplies or natural resources, *will* know who's to blame. Then, they might recall Pogo's words, "We met the enemy, and he is us."

Chapter 6

THE SILVERTIP'S SALVATION—A STRATEGY

In the face of severe exploitation of grizzly country, it's tempting to write off the wilderness king. However, this would be tragically premature. America can still retain a self-sustaining grizzly population south of Canada.

Most efforts to save the silvertip end up, sooner or later, in a federal agency's hands, since most grizzly habitat lies on federal land administered by the Forest Service, the Bureau of Land Management, or the National Park Service. These are *public* agencies responsible to *public* demands and charged with protecting *public* values on *public* lands. Since the grizzly represents a *public* resource of insurmountable significance, *public* agencies should bend to *public* pressure and put the bear first in land use decisions. However, federal agencies — particularly the Forest Service — aren't giving the grizzly the priority the bear needs to survive.

AS THE WILDERNESS GOES, SO GOES THE GRIZZLY

It isn't possible to overstate the importance of protecting remaining grizzly habitat. Simply stated, the lower 48 states will lose the grizzly without these

143

remote regions. Or as Andy Russell put it, "As surely as the sun rises tomorrow morning, grizzly country is wilderness country, and he cannot live without it."

Habitat protection isn't the only solution, but it's the cornerstone of any program to save the bear. Without shoring up the last refuges, all other efforts to save the silvertip suffer. To have a wild, free-roaming grizzly population, the lower 48 states must first provide the bear with a secure foundation — a viable habitat.

In discussing this idea, Dr. John Craighead advised caution in broadcasting the urgency of wild land preservation. "You could end up with all the habitat in the world and no grizzly bears," he warned. He is right, of course. Without basic biological research, bureaucratic responsibility, public tolerance, close regulation of hunting, scientific unity, and a few more "musts," the grizzly could disappear regardless of the amount of quality habitat available. Nonetheless, preservation of the grizzly must start with preservation of the remaining habitat. As the wilderness goes, so goes the grizzly.

Luckily, citizens have some potent tools to protect this vital habitat, not the least of which is the Wilderness Act of 1964, which created the Wilderness Preservation System. Already, several sizeable slices of grizzly country have received some protection under this system. However, much of the bear's remaining habitat sits without any security. Most of this unprotected habitat lies on federal lands, but as Chapter 5 illustrates, this hardly means it's safe. Many of these lands are *de facto* wilderness, possessing wilderness characteristics but lacking the protection of official designation under the Wilderness Act.

The Wilderness Act required the Forest Service, the U.S. Fish and Wildlife Service, and the National Park Service to review all roadless areas for possible inclusion in the Wilderness Preservation System. But, in general, insufficient recognition was given to wilderness values.

National Park Service officials at Glacier and Yellowstone parks recommended most park lands for wilderness. But these lands already had considerable protection. True, wilderness status added security from commercial development common in both Parks and discouraged future policy changes which could go against the grizzly. Nonetheless, designation of most of the two national parks as wilderness did little to change the grizzly's future.

The Forest Service, on the other hand, recommended only a bare minimum for wilderness, leaving large portions of the grizzly's domain open to "multiple use," which means the area will probably be logged or

144

otherwise developed. Although wilderness qualifies for "multiple use" management, according to FS regulations, in practice the agency considers wilderness as "single use" land.

Generally speaking, the FS picked only tree-bare highlands as wilderness excluding areas with timber, mineral, mechanized recreation, or other commercial values. Unfortunately, these excluded areas, which are often the lowlands, are vital to wildlife, including the grizzly.

A good example is the Taylor-Hilgard area, northwest of Yellowstone Park. The FS had the opportunity to join 245,000 acres of prime grizzly country to the 113,102-acre Spanish Peaks Primitive Area. Instead, the FS designated only a few smaller pieces from the larger area as wilderness and left a corridor between them and the Spanish Peaks. (Refer to Chapter 5.) In short, the agency vetoed wilderness designation for land with commercial potential. This area is now seriously threatened by proposals for new roads, power lines, logging, and resort development.

Montanans protested this action, but objections went unanswered. So Senator Lee Metcalf (D-Montana), a friend of the grizzly, became concerned. In January 1975, he introduced the Montana Wilderness Study Bill, which would protect the entire Taylor-Hilgard region and eight other smaller areas in Montana, several of which support — or could support — grizzlies. This bill awards wplderness status to these nine areas while an intensive five-year study is conducted, and after five years, some of them may be recommended for wilderness. Remaining consistent, the FS sided with commercial interests in opposing this wilderness study legislation.

The FS repeated this performance with the fragile Absaroka/Beartooth area, northeast of Yellowstone Park. Despite near-unanimous support from the public — including Montana Governor Thomas L. Judge — for the largest possible wilderness, the FS recommended for wilderness little more than one-half of the Absaroka/Beartooth. In the process, the agency again left important grizzly habitat open to destruction.

Idaho's proposed River of No Return Wilderness, which has a great potential for re-establishing a grizzly population, was likewise undermined by the FS. And in northwestern Montana along the Middle Fork of the Flathead River, the proposed Great Bear Wilderness — appropriately named after its outstanding inhabitant — lies unprotected between Glacier Park and the Bob Marshall Wilderness, because the FS has failed to consider it for wilderness. In frustration, conservationists have asked Congress to add all of these areas to the Wilderness Preservation System, an action opposed by the FS.

145

The timber industry joins the FS in opposing most wilderness proposals. And loggers have been successful in stymieing congressional and citizen efforts to protect grizzly habitat — both by direct protest and by encouraging the FS to either oppose wilderness or allow development of wild lands. Conservationists say it's foolish to break open any more virgin country when at least 90% of the lower 48 states has already been roaded — and especially if the area supports a grizzly population. But timbermen don't hold this view, as logging roads and clearcuts extend ever deeper into Old Ephraim's kingdom.

Actually, many of the areas already mentioned (and others the big bear needs) have minimal value as timber. Still, the timber companies won't tolerate wilderness designations. At times, it seems they are blindly opposing the wilderness concept, believing it foolish to preserve any additional wild land.

Certainly, there can be more careful and productive management of the millions of acres of forest land already roaded. But unfortunately, forestry budgets appear to run counter to this goal — most funds go to cutting, leaving little for reforestation and long-term management.

Also, the allowable cut often exceeds the forest's ability to renew itself. Sustained-yield management should keep a continuous flow of wood products coming from the timberland — *forever.* By overcutting, foresters hurry the day when Americans must turn back to the cutover land for another crop, only to find it missing. This mismanagement may meet short-term economic objectives, but it ignores the future.

Timber company officials think about the future, but their opinions hardly mix with the feelings of anyone hoping to preserve grizzlies. The view of Angelo J. Mancini, general manager of Star Studs Co., a western Wyoming lumber firm, represents typical timber company policy. In his official comment on the Department of the Interior's classification of the grizzly as a threatened species, Mancini wrote: "If this course of Holy Grail chasing is allowed to continue as it has in the recent past, then it will only be a short span before we will have the United States set aside for Wilderness and Wildlife, and man will be the most endangered of all the poor dumb animals."

Granted, there is legitimate demand for timber products which must be met. But consumption at the present rate results in overcutting and loss of virgin country. Americans can have a continuous supply of wood products without losing the grizzly on much of the bear's remaining range.

In fairness, the timber industry is hardly alone in opposing the protection

146

of grizzly habitat. Mining associations, sheepmen, stockgrowers, business groups, ski resort developers, and off-road vehicle clubs have joined arms with the timber lords in an attempt to kill wilderness legislation.

The Idaho Mining Association, for example, labels people hoping to preserve wilderness "wildernuts." They are, the mining companies say, a few radicals who want to fill the West with "no-no" areas that nobody will ever use.

At a recent meeting of the Montana Stockgrowers at Big Sky, Montana, delegates forcefully opposed Metcalf's wilderness study bill and his effort to protect the Great Bear Wilderness. Then, someone mentioned that Metcalf had another wilderness bill. Upon hearing this, a delegate jumped up shouting, "Great, let's find that one and oppose it, too." Hearty laughter followed — for the grizzly, a not-so-humorous sign of the times.

THE ENDANGERED SPECIES ACT

The second major tool for protecting grizzly habitat, the Endangered Species Act of 1973 (ESA), is still young and, as yet, not fully understood. Much will depend on how the courts interpret this law. However, preliminary appraisals by some legal students deem it potentially more powerful than the National Environmental Policy Act, which is widely acclaimed as today's most far-reaching environmental legislation.

Briefly, the ESA sets up guidelines for designation of threatened and endangered animals and plants, and provides for protection of critical habitat. It also allows citizen suits to help enforce the Act.

After nearly two years of public effort on behalf of the grizzly, the ESA's administrative agency, the U.S. Fish and Wildlife Service (U.S. Department of the Interior) officially classified the grizzly bear as a threatened species, on September 1, 1975. This paved the way for protection of critical grizzly habitat.

Then, attention was turned to perhaps the most noteworthy part of the new law, the already celebrated "Section 7." It's short, but potentially explosive:

> Sec. 7. The Secretary [of the Interior] shall review other programs administered by him and utilize such programs in furtherance of the purposes of this Act. All other Federal departments and agencies shall, in consultation with and with the assistance of the Secretary, utilize their authorities in furtherance of the purposes of this Act by carrying out programs for the conservation of endangered species and threatened

147

species listed pursuant to section 4 of this Act and by taking such action necessary to insure that actions authorized, funded, or carried out by them do not jeopardize the continued existence of such endangered species and threatened species or result in the destruction or modification of habitat or of such species which is determined by the Secretary, after consultation as appropriate with the affected States, to be critical.

Of course, much depends on exactly what "critical" habitat is. Is *all* remaining habitat of a threatened species "critical"? If not, what part is? Presently, wildlife officials are trying — with little success — to define this evasive adjective. Grizzly advocates urge that all remaining habitat be "critical." At the other end of the pole, the FS and developers argue for a bare minimum. For example, of about 12 million acres of "occupied" grizzly habitat in Montana, the FS feels that only about 1.5 million acres are "critical," most of this area within already established wilderness areas like the Bob Marshall and Cabinet Mountains.

Many biologists want the designation of critical habitat to wait until they know exactly what "critical" means. And state game departments generally support the same position.

In the Rocky Mountain West, the designation of critical habitat has created a hot controversy. Even the Wyoming Wildlife Federation has passed a resolution opposing critical habitat designation, although its parent organization, the National Wildlife Federation has favored putting the grizzly on the threatened list. Furthermore, the Wyoming Wildlife Federation members want the bear removed from the threatened list. Wyoming residents worry that a "critical" habitat designation will cut back on traditional uses of the national forests around Yellowstone Park — hunting, camping, dude ranching, logging, dirt biking, snowmobiling, etc.

Actually, a cutback in hunting seems to be the big concern in Wyoming. The ESA contains a provision for "look alike" species. This means that if hunting a threatened or endangered animal is banned or curtailed, taking a species that looks like the protected animal may also be stopped. Since the black bear has a brown color phase and young grizzlies are often difficult to differentiate from black bears, sportsmen fear an end to black bear hunting.

"It is our feeling that no need has been shown for a critical habitat designation for the grizzly." James M. Borzea, President of the Wyoming Wildlife Federation, wrote to former Interior Secretary Kleppe. "A critical habitat designation anywhere outside of Yellowstone National Park would be a futile attempt at providing habitat for one species while totally ignoring all other game species and recreational interests. The wandering

148

characteristic of the grizzly would seem to dictate that this bear could be found in much of our low country as well as our high mountain areas. Thus, any critical habitat area would seem to be impractical as well as detrimental."

Ironically, in the same letter, Borzea wrote, "Our organization is very concerned about the future of the grizzly bear."

The Wyoming Wildlife Federation (through the Cody County Sportsman's Club) also prepared a brochure soliciting opposition to the designation of critical habitat and funds to help the club oppose it. The brochure reads: "What can occur in a 'critical habitat area?' Condemnation of private lands. Closure and removal of lodges, dude ranches, and campground facilities. Closing to all hunting. Closure to fishing, hiking, and trail-riding within the area."

Such scare tactics and unrealistic exaggerations kept westerners stirred up. Even frequent efforts by federal officials to illustrate how such extreme results of critical habitat designation were impossible failed to quiet these fears.

So on November 5, 1976, when the U.S. Fish and Wildlife Service came up with a draft proposal to designate almost 13 million acres of Idaho, Montana, Washington, and Wyoming as critical habitat, the public comment went strongly against the plan. Miners, outfitters, loggers, dirt bikers, woolgrowers, four-wheel-drive clubs, cattlemen, businessmen, state game departments, resort developers, state legislatures, western congressmen, and just about everybody else opposed this "broad brush" approach to critical habitat. Many protesters favored no critical habitat, and others wanted it restricted to national parks, wilderness areas, and primitive areas where most commercial development is prohibited anyway.

The field hearings on the proposal were depressing for participants favoring protection of critical habitat. The rooms were packed with hundreds of people, most of whom angrily blasted critical habitat delineation.

"A great deal has been said about the danger of being caught between a grizzly and her cubs," Don Aldrich summarized public reaction to the critical habitat proposal when testifying at a Missoula, Montana hearing. "Unbiased evaluation cannot help but conclude that it is much more dangerous to be caught between *Homo sapiens* and the nickel."

Most of the other testimony verified Aldrich's prediction. For example, Charlie Shaw, a former forest ranger from the Flathead National Forest, knocked preservationists who, in his opinion, want to protect the grizzly at "our" expense. "They want no oil prospecting, no mining, no hydro-

149

electric sites, no nothing. All they want is wilderness and they can't live in it or gain any benefit from it except to look at it. That's a complete waste of natural resources." Later in the hearing, Larry Watts, a forester from Libby, Montana agreed by noting: "I'm getting to the point where I prefer people instead of environmentalists."

And these are only two comments from a steady stream of adverse views of the critical habitat proposal. Many comments were gross overreactions to a sincere effort to preserve America's big bear — attitudes often stemming from entrenched resentment to the federal bureaucracy and national conservation groups. It's also harsh testimony to the need for national pressure to preserve the grizzly, as local sentiment usually goes against the bear.

Chapter 5 also contained harsh testimony, evidence of what is happening to the grizzly's last habitat. Now that the nation has a workable, practical method of declaring some of the disappearing habitat "critical" and thus preventing overuse or development, the western states violently oppose such action.

The U.S. Fish and Wildlife Service has repeatedly guaranteed sportsmen that hunting will not be banned. Yet, in blind fear of the federal government, the hunters of western states don't believe it. Experts like Dr. Charles Jonkel have publicly stated that cutbacks in hiking, hunting, camping, etc. are not part of critical habitat designation. But paranoia still runs rampant.

Without naming much of the present and potential grizzly habitat "critical," the effectiveness of the Endangered Species Act, whose purpose is to protect rare species and their habitat, seriously suffers. By restricting such designation to places like Yellowstone Park, the purpose is defeated. (Yellowstone Park already has the protection of park policies and wilderness status.) Critical habitat designation is a means by which *unprotected* habitat can be protected. Obviously, to secure a meaningful delineation of critical habitat, conservationists *nationwide* must mount the same level of campaign they did to force the Interior Department to designate the grizzly as a threatened species in the first place.

Regardless of what compromise ultimately emerges, however, the decision may go to the courts. This means the courts will define "critical" habitat, leaving a sour taste with wildlife professionals, who feel the definition should result from biological process.

How will the ESA affect the developments mentioned in Chapter 5? Nobody knows. Perhaps all of them violate the law. Most likely, the courts will rule against some of them. Time will tell.

Certainly, the ESA won't stop all development of federal lands, as some critics claim. However, it will undoubtedly have a profound impact on federal land use policies, which should benefit the grizzly.

Logging is a case in point. Grizzly experts say timbering can have a neutral or beneficial impact on the big bears — *if* planned and conducted properly. Therefore, the ESA won't halt all timber sales on public lands, as some timber industry representatives charge.

Federal agencies — and in the grizzly's case, particularly the FS — will have to obey this law. If they don't, they will spend inordinate time and money defending themselves against citizens who keep dragging them into court for jeopardizing the threatened grizzly or his critical habitat. Notably, Section 11 of the ESA allows fines of up to $20,000 and imprisonment of up to one year per violation for federal employees who violate the law.

Preferably, federal agencies would voluntarily obey the Endangered Species Act, so underfunded citizens' groups won't be forced to initiate litigation. Nonetheless, it will probably take a few stiff fines to prompt strict adherence to the Endangered Species Act.

NEW HOMES FOR GRIZZLIES

Dear Sir:

I sincerely hope you are against any transplanting of grizzly bears from Nat'l Parks to our Nat'l Forests. In my work I run into many black bears every year and do not mind, in fact enjoy seeing them, but I don't want to see any "Park Bears," black or grizzly, for as you know, they have no fear of people, and we who tramp the woods today don't carry rifles, as our frontiersmen did. Anyway, I want to assure you that I and many other people who I have heard talking do not want any bear transplants.

"Well, maybe it wasn't such a good idea after all." Perhaps that was what a few Idaho public servants were thinking in 1970, when an angry citizenry challenged their tentative grizzly transplant plan with letters like the one above.

Professional wildlife managers and/or grizzly admirers have had to consider the following facts:

1. Grizzly populations are sparse or declining.

2. Idaho, Montana, Wyoming, and other western states have millions of acres of public land that historically supported grizzlies, but now are void of the big bears.

3. Yellowstone Park officials were urging western states to accept sur-

151

plus grizzlies and attempt to re-establish lost populations in suitable habitat.

Park Service heavyweights, who felt like blind men walking through quicksand flats because of an ever-increasing number of controversial bear/man conflicts occurring after the dumps had been closed, didn't know which way to jump. Officials live-trapped grizzlies in the campgrounds and tourist centers regularly, but there was no place to put them. Moving them deep into this park didn't solve the problem; the bears often beat the ranger back to the campground where the trapping had occurred. Even bears transplanted into national forests bordering the park sometimes returned to the campgrounds. Only a few of the bears could be destroyed without arousing a public outcry. In search of a safe spot to jump, therefore, the National Park Service (NPS) urgently asked states to consider transplanting grizzlies into suitable habitat away from the park.

On April 1, 1970, Superintendent Jack Anderson wrote to several states emphasizing that the park's "first priority" was re-establishing grizzlies in "suitable historical habitats" and asking for cooperation in a transplant plan. And for one of the few times in history, plenty of grizzlies were available for such an effort.

Apparently, Idaho was the first taker. Wildlifers from the Idaho Fish and Game Department, the NPS, and the Forest Service hastily pounded out a plan to transplant 18 grizzlies into the Priest Lake country in northern Idaho. They hoped to reinforce the area's struggling grizzly population and at the same time prevent bears from being killed "administratively" in and around Yellowstone Park.

An official agreement between the NPS and the Idaho Fish and Game Department was mutually approved, with the FS concurring. The agencies were preparing to test the plan in public waters when word leaked out, rumors spreading like wildfire.

Public reaction was more frequent and potent than anyone expected. In fact, today the Idaho Fish and Game Department doesn't like to talk about the transplant idea — initially sidestepping inquiries with "just a rumor that got going a few years ago." After further questioning, however, they admit such a program had been considered.

It's easy to understand why the department doesn't eagerly volunteer information about the plan. As one FS official put it, "The public got hold of it, and then all hell broke loose."

It must have been tense around Fish and Game Department and FS offices with public sentiment running like this:

152

• I have five grandchildren all under six years old. If the Forest Service and Park officials are allowed to plant Grizzly Bears in the Priest Lake country, I cannot take any of these children in that area and feel they are safe. There is no justifiable reason for planting Grizzlies in the area that we are trying to preserve for our children and grandchildren to enjoy.

• Priest Lake area is now safe for people to visit and enjoy but if it is stocked with Grizzlies, it will be unsafe. Look at Yellowstone Park, with all its supervision there are many people crippled or killed each year. I ask you as my Senator, to prevent this transplant...I believe that I know what I am talking about as I lived 10 years up the Bull River out of Noxon, Montana, next to the Cabinet Wilderness which is infested with Grizzlies...."

• Why don't you tell the Park Service to take care of their own bears and not to dump them on us. Grizzlies are always dangerous and I believe we should have designated areas for them within the Nat'l Parks, but not just anyplace within the Nat'l Forests. I quote from a report of a well-known wilderness traveler after a trip in the Bob Marshall [Wilderness Area] "It was a very pleasant trip except for the ever present possibility of encountering an angry grizzly."

• Inasmuch as the area in which the animals are to be released is used extensively for camping, picnicking and fishing as well as berry picking, and since the presence of grizzlies in the area would greatly curtail our use as such of this area, we [The Board of County Commissioners] respectfully request that you exert whatever authority you may have in stopping the release of the grizzlies in our county.

• Please accept this letter as the official protest of the Idaho Cattlemen's Association in regards to the transplanting of grizzly bears from the Yellowstone Park area into the upper Priest Lake area in the Selkirk Mountains. The cattle industry urges that this movement of grizzly bears be cancelled immediately.

• We are homeowners in the Priest Lake area and are very disturbed that grizzly bears are to be planted at the upper Priest Lake area and wish you would do what you can to stop this.

• In regards to the report that you are considering the release of grizzlies in the upper Priest Lake area, let us urge that you not do this. We are very upset at this report for several reasons:
1. We don't want grizzlies there!
2. Grizzlies have already taken over large areas of the West. Yellowstone and Glacier are examples of the very worst in grizzly management and to our thought have been completely ruined for human use. Between what we read and the reports of friends

153

on the scene, we won't go near either.
3. We want this area kept in a usable condition for us and future generations.

• If you want to preserve the species, why not put them in a zoo of sorts, using natural habitat like they are doing in Florida? I'm sure you wouldn't want to worry about your grandchpldren playing in your yard. Priest Lake is a beautiful place — let's keep it that way. We don't want episodes like they are having at Yellowstone.

These excerpts have been drawn from only a few of the letters Idaho residents sent to the Forest Service, the Park Service, the Fish and Game Department, the Governor, and the Congressional delegation. In view of typical bureaucratic operation, it came as no surprise that the plan was dropped. As Roger Bumsted of the Region I Forester's office noted, "The people got so obnoxious that there was nothing to do but drop the proposal."

Apparently, most people commenting on the proposal thought wildlife managers were preparing to secretly haul "problem" grizzlies from Yellowstone Park and dump them indiscriminately in other areas without study or public consideration. This was not the case. Public officials had planned to monitor the bears via telemetry and closely evaluate the transplant area. "People didn't realize we were going to keep a tight rein on this," recalls Ray Rodgers, supervisor of the Idaho Panhandle National Forest. "The bears were going to be monitored and if it looked like there would be a problem, we'd be on it right now." Also, habitual campground or "dump" bears that had been involved in property damage weren't acceptable as transplants.

Officials had also been planning a full information campaign before the transplant. In fact, a few agencies and sportsman clubs had already been informed of the tentative plan. "No opposition or adverse criticism came from these groups," an FS inter-agency memo described reaction.

But for unknown reasons, people still conjured up visions of helicopters dropping misbehaving grizzlies into their front yards. They reacted negatively, killing the proposal.

Wyoming also tried the transplant plan. Again, the FS, MPS, and Wyoming Game and Fish Department agreed to transplant grizzlies (15 bears) into the Teton Wilderness, southeast of the park. One bear (a 600 pound male) was released near Crater Lake in 1971. Unfortunately, the bear showed up in an outfitter's camp about two days after the release. The campers complained, and the FS reacted, prohibiting any further transplants.

Wyoming, however, plans to continue transplanting. In 1974, two bears were fitted with radio transmitters and released in the North Absaroka Wilderness. One died in a fall down a talus slope a day or so after it was released. (Observers concluded it was attempting to return to the park.) The other bear successfully denned in the area.

Montana also tried transplanting bears with some success. During 1970-71, the Montana Department of Fish and Game worked out an agreement with the FS stipulating several transplant sites within the Gallatin National Forest. During those 2 years, 19 bears were released. However, only 4 survived.

Predictably, Montana also took sharp criticism, with this sheepman's comment typical of local sentiment: "Most of the people living in the area do not want bears transplanted into the area." (In spite of adverse reaction, Montana and Wyoming continued the transplant operation on a limited basis within the Yellowstone Park vicinity.)

The transplant issue is certainly one of the most perplexing parts of the grizzly story. Everywhere one turns for answers, he finds more questions.

In the first place, the hurried transplant plans sprouting from the Park Service's dilemma of 1970-71 were poorly conceived, their faults outweighing their merits. However, no single person or agency deserves the blame, which rests primarily with the difficulty of the situation.

Regardless of the merits of a rapid closing of Yellowstone's garbage dumps, they had, in fact, been closed, and the park had problem bears. The sticky question of what to do with these problem bears — which probably should have been, in biological terms, "removed from the population" — remained unanswered. If moved back in the park or to nearby forests, the bears soon returned. And the public wouldn't accept killing them or transplanting them to other wilderness regions.

Transplanting bears seemed like a viable solution, but the concept became tainted when the NPS tried to remove "garbage bears" from Yellowstone. Although every park bear isn't a problem bear, no one could deny that a problem bear in the park might be a problem bear anywhere. Certainly, the public believed that all park bears were unpredictable and dangerous.

Liability became another problem of transplanting bears. After a court found the National Park Service liable for a Tom Walker's death,[1] public officials became even more spooky about moving bears from one area to another. What happened in Wyoming testifies to official nervousness about transplants. In 1970 Wyoming had agreements signed to release 15 bears.

[1]See Chapter 4 for details in the Walker case.

Future
Grizzly Country?

The grizzly's future would be substantially strengthened with a series of successful transplants into historic habitats where the big bear was exterminated. Yes, such a program is riddled with problems and controversy. But nonetheless, it's possible and should remain a high priority management option. These are only three of the many areas with potential for such a transplant.

Selway/Bitterroot Wilderness. Tom McBride photo.

Proposed River of No Return Wilderness. Ted Trueblood photo.

Gila Wilderness. Forest Service photo.

158

They released one, which tore up a camp. The FS then said "no more." In 1972, Wyoming released two bears and had agreements and plans to plant five more. Suddenly, the FS said "no" again.

Larry Roop, who surpervised the Wyoming transplants, had a positive experience. Benefiting from knowledge of Idaho's explosive response to rumor, Roop emphasized openness in his operation. After a full-fledged information effort, the transplants came off without public backlash. "You must stop the rumors," Roop stressed. "We didn't even get a clipping in the local newspaper." (However, they did get a bad reaction from the FS, which stopped the Wyoming transplant program.)

Considering the circumstances, why should officials transplant grizzlies from the Yellowstone "ecosystem" at all? Bears can expand into areas near the park, if they are indeed suitable habitat. No physical barriers (like urban areas) prevent this, and many of the transplant sites have grizzlies already.

To date, transplant efforts have *not* been intended to re-establish a new population in an area unoccupied by grizzlies. Instead, wildlife managers hope to "save some bears from being disposed of," as Roop puts it, and to perfect transplant techniques. With better control, a real transplant into an area like the Selway/Bitterroot, Gila, or River of No Return Wildernesses (see table on page 160) has a better chance of succeeding. Since such areas don't have a direct line to a viable grizzly population, they will never have grizzlies without a transplant.

When and if a real transplant is tried, it must be done right. First, carefully study the area to determine if the habitat is suitable and how many grizzlies are required to create a viable population. Next, conduct a *complete* public information campaign to win approval of the plan. Then — *and only then* — introduce wild grizzlies into the area. Finally, closely monitor the bears for the first few years to determine success and to watch for possible man/bear conflicts.

In July 1975, the FS released a management plan for the Selway/ Bitterroot Wilderness that left the way open for grizzly transplants. Commendably, in suggesting this future option, the FS stressed the need for public education and research.

When the day comes to try it, however, there will undoubtedly be controversy. Public servants must be prepared to "take some heat" and "stick to their guns" for the grizzly's sake. If they have made every effort to inform the public, have majority support to back them up, and have gathered the necessary research data, they must follow through, no matter how difficult the situation becomes.

159

GRIZZLY HABITAT SUMMARY

(HABITAT PROPOSED FOR INCLUSION IN THE WILDERNESS PRESERVATION SYSTEM[1])

Area	State	Acres	Location	Has Grizzlies[2]	Could Have
Spanish Peaks Wilderness	Montana	113,102	Gallatin NF	yes	
Aldo Leopold	New Mexico	231,737	Gila NF		yes
Beartooth Wilderness	Montana & Wyoming	960,00	Custer, Gallatin, & Shoshone NFs	yes	
River of No Return Wilderness	Idaho & Montana	2,320,688	Boise, Challis, Salmon, Payette, Nezperce, & Bitterroot NFs		yes
Taylor/Hilgard Wilderness	Montana	245,000	Beaverhead & Gallatin NFs	yes	
Hyalite/Porcupine/ Buffalo Horn Wilderness	Montana	163,000	Gallatin NF	yes	
Blue Range Wilderness	Arizona & New Mexico	231,300	Apache NF		yes
Ten Lakes Wilderness	Montana	30,000	Kootenai NF	yes	
Centennial Mtns. Primitive Area	Idaho & Montana	40,000	BLM land west of Yellowstone Natl. Park	yes	
Gila Wilderness Additions	New Mexico	181,228	Gila NF		yes
Rocky Mountain Natl. Park	Colorado	248,000	central Colorado		yes
Scotchman Peaks Wilderness	Idaho & Montana	140,000	Kottenai & Panhandle NFs	yes	
Popo Agie Wilderness	Wyoming	162,000	Shoshone NF	yes	
Bob Marshall Wilderness Additions	Montana	223,491	Flathead, Lolo, & Lewis and Clark NFs	yes	
Scapegoat Wilderness Additions	Montana	39,100	Helena & Lewis and Clark NFs	yes	

[1]These are the citizens' proposals, not those recommended by the Forest Service or other federal agencies. These agencies left much of these vital grizzly habitats open to development. For more information on any of these proposals, write Clif Merritt, Western Regional Office, The Wilderness Society, 4260 E. Evans, Denver, CO 80022.

(HABITAT ALREADY PROTECTED AS WILDERNESS AREAS OR PARKS)

Area	State	Acres	Location	Has Grizzlies[2]	Could Have
Gila Wilderness	New Mexico	438,626	Gila NF		yes
North Absaroka Wilderness	Wyoming	351,104	Shoshone NF	yes	
Teton Wilderness	Wyoming	557,311	Bridger/Teton NF	yes	
Mission Mountains Wilderness	Montana	75,588	Flathead NF	yes	
Selway/Bitterroot Wilderness	Idaho & Montana	1,240,618	Bitterroot, Nezperce, Lolo, & Clearwater NFs		yes
Anaconda/Pintlar Wilderness	Montana	159,086	Beaverhead, Deer Lodge, & Bitterroot NFs		yes
Scapegoat Wilderness	Montana	240,000	Helena, Lolo, & Lewis and Clark NFs	yes	
Cabinet Wilderness	Montana	94,272	Kootenai NF	yes	
Glacier Natl. Park	Montana	1,013,129	northwestern Montana	yes	
Yellowstone Natl. Park	Idaho, Montana, & Wyoming	2,221,773	northwestern Wyoming	yes	
Grand Teton Natl. Park	Wyoming	310,443	northwestern Wyoming	yes	
North Cascades Natl. Park	Washington	505,000	northeastern Washington	yes	
Washaki Wilderness	Wyoming	691,130	Shoshone NF	yes	
Bridger Wilderness	Wyoming	392,100	Bridger/Teton NF		yes
Weminuche Wilderness	Colorado	405,031	San Juan NF		yes
Flattops Wilderness	Colorado	235,230	White River & Routt NFs		yes
Fitzpatrick Wilderness	Wyoming	191,103	Shoshone NF	yes	

[2]The area's capability to support grizzly bears is tentative and certainly subject to error. However, it was based on the opinions of professional wildlife managers throughout the West. Many large roadless areas aren't included because authorities feel they lack potential for re-establishing grizzly populations — even though they historically supported the big bear. And some of the areas listed here as possible transplant sites will most likely be ruled out after careful research.

Will a true transplant program ever be operative? One prime area is now being actively considered for such a program. However, officials have asked that specifics be avoided. They strongly agree with a full information campaign. "But we aren't ready yet," they claim. If they can successfully carry out this particular program, the public may accept further transplants.

A single successful transplant operation would do much to relieve a major stumbling block in the grizzly's path to survival — public intolerance. Acceptance of Old Ephraim, rather than hate and fear of the big bear, would mark a giant step toward preserving the species.

RESEARCH

As the transplant controversy illustrates, hardly anything can be done for the grizzly without a well-funded, well-publicized, and extensive research program. Indeed, research is the backbone of all wildlife management. Without the necessary evidence to back up management programs, administrators can't justify them.

This hard fact came home to the Montana and Wyoming game departments during the controversy over designating the grizzly a threatened species. Biologists were sure that management prescriptions would benefit the bear, but they couldn't completely prove their thesis. They had information, but not *enough* to convince an inquisitive public. Subsequently, people didn't believe the departments were giving the grizzly adequate protection, so they urged the federal government to take over.

Organizations committed to preserving the grizzly must be committed to research, and this committment will have to be backed with funds. When Dr. Charles Jonkel was organizing his study in northwestern Montana, he wrote to the citizen groups that were pushing for a ban on grizzly hunting and asked for funds, but he received meager financial support.[1]

Without knowing the bear's biology, management is difficult — if not impossible. And the grizzly, with his size, diverse habitat, strength, mobility, and disposition, is particularly hard to study. Thus, an extra effort becomes necessary, as only research can unravel the riddles of the big bear's behavior and habitat.

---

[1]Of the ten groups listed in the footnote on page 49, the National Wildlife Federation contributed $2,000, the New York Zoological Society $3,000 and the Animal Protection Institute $500.

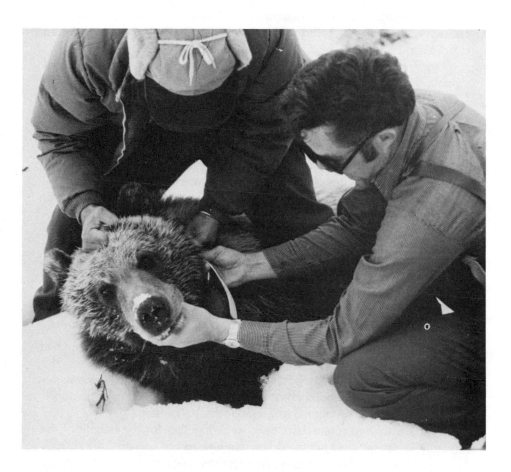

Researchers, such as these from the Interagency Study Team working in the Yellowstone National Park area, live trap grizzlies and then release them after attaching tags, markers, and at times, radio transmitters so the bear's activities can be monitored. Without knowing the basics of grizzly behavior and habitat, management recommendations remain riddled with questions. Interagency Study Team photo.

Unfortunately, most research data available today comes from atypical grizzly populations — the garbage-foraging bears of Yellowstone and the salmon-feeding bears along Alaskan rivers. Many professionals are reluctant to apply this information to a population such as exists in northwestern Montana.

Worst of all, widespread and destructive development of private and public grizzly habitat proceeds without this basic biological information. Private land managers have a moral responsibility to analyze current and pending grizzly research projects before extensively developing their property. And public administrators are both morally and legally obligated to study such research before proceeding. But neither the private land managers nor the public administrators are waiting for research.

Researchers will undoubtedly find critical areas. However, under the present situation, a road, timber sale, resort, mine, etc. could destroy one or more of these vital areas without land managers realizing what was happening. However, if a region were thoroughly studied before development, damage could be avoided by modifying or denying some — but not all — commercial ventures. Without such control, the grizzly will eventually disappear from the cumulative impact of error after error.

SCIENTIFIC UNITY AND BUREAUCRATIC RESPONSIBILITY

The Yellowstone feud was ridiculous, understandably creating public concern over the fate of the Yellowstone grizzly. As biologists bickered, the bear suffered. Scientific cooperation collapsed during the Yellowstone debate, and attempts to build up or destroy personalities seriously damaged efforts to preserve a national treasure — the Yellowstone grizzly.

All agencies and researchers must work together for the benefit of the grizzly. The parks must permit independent research — even if the conclusions conflict with existing policy. And scientific cooperation must be given the utmost respect.

FIRE CONTROL

Perhaps an overemphasis on forest fire suppression has lowered the quality of grizzly habitat. Jonkel wonders about this: "Recent experiments in allowing fires to burn naturally in parks show potential for increasing the grizzly's food source."

Game managers have proved that tight fire control has "closed up" forests by gradually allowing conifers to reclaim the open areas, which are important to big game. For example, Idaho wildlife managers are actually burning forests to improve elk range.

The FS and other agencies are grudgingly moving from "all forest fires are bad" policy promoted by Smokey Bear to a new science, fire ecology. Allowing fires to burn, in some areas and under particular circumstances, may improve the West's ability to raise grizzly bears.

AGREEMENTS WITH INDIAN RESERVATIONS

Federal lands aside, western Indian reservations probably control more grizzly habitat than any other landowner. Right now, no regulations or grizzly management programs exist on these reservations.

In 1974, 75% of Montana's nonhunting grizzly loss (mortality and the removal of live cubs from the population) occurred on Indian reservations — 15 of 20 bears. Additional losses probably went unreported.

Also, inroads into grizzly habitat on tribal lands continue without regulation. In fact, nobody knows how serious habitat encroachment is on the reservations.

Hopefully, wildlife managers and Indian tribes can work together to properly manage grizzlies and life-giving habitat of the reservations.

TOURISM POLICIES

Most western states actively promote national visitation through a state-funded travel promotion bureau. Regardless of its economic advantages or disadvantages, this practice increases human use of delicate grizzly ranges. Worse, tourism indirectly encourages road building, recreational land sales, resource extraction, and other development of vital habitat.

Montana ad agencies promote the state nationally as "the last of the big time splendors." It wouldn't be so *splendid* if this policy helped rob Montana of its most splendid wild animal.

MINING LAWS

Several archaic mining laws and regulations such as the Mining Law of 1872 and the Mineral Leasing Act of 1920 have repeatedly resisted revision or revocation. These laws encourage open-ended exploitation of the public lands and *must be rewritten.* Congress has made several false starts on this needed action, but the mining lobby has continually frustrated concerned congressmen.

LIMIT TO WILDERNESS USE

In the future, public land managers may restrict visitation to wilderness areas. This has already happened in some parks, and it will eventually come to most parks and wilderness areas. However, hikers aren't likely to object, if fewer backcountry visits will help perpetuate the wilderness king.

LAND USE PLANNING

"Land use planning" is a phrase that public officials, conservationists, politicians, and developers now toss around indiscriminately. But "land use planning" has, under certain circumstances, been detrimental to the grizzly. When planning becomes a method by which incompatible development in an inappropriate area can be justified, the concept falls apart. However, if planning principles can be used to properly regulate development, then — and only then — can they be powerful tools in helping preserve the grizzly and other natural amenities.

The Ski Yellowstone proposal and the Big Sky development (Chapter 5) offer excellent examples of negative aspects of "land use planning." Both are "well-planned" by the developer's definition. True, within the development's boundaries, every square inch has a specific purpose, and the developers have colorful maps to illustrate their plan. However, developers don't look past the front gate — *the far-reaching, indirect, incremental, and uncontrollable impact on the entire area isn't considered.* After a large, unwieldy development such as Big Sky goes in, spin off development is difficult, if not impossible, to control without strict areawide planning. Scenic mountain valleys need comprehensive areawide plans *before* large developments are approved.   Often the big resorts *want* these comprehensive plans and zoning restrictions, hoping to close the door after their development wins approval. This policy reduces competition and public resentment, since spin-off development is reduced. Therefore, even if a developer's push for areawide plans may be self-serving, local residents should join in backing sound and comprehensive planning. In fact, large developments should never be approved without such a comprehensive plan in effect. In Big Sky's case, the resort made a substantial commitment to plan the valley, but the local residents said "no."

Resistance to change is strong in the West, and rural property rights are close to a westerner's heart. Any plan that could jeopardize these rights is immediately suspect and stands little chance of voter approval.

For these reasons, "land use planning" in the Rocky Mountain West has been little more than a token effort. Local residents — and particularly ranchers — want things "left like they are." Yet, they won't accept restrictions such as those of a good comprehensive plan. Unfortunately, their life style will disappear before their very eyes without strict planning.

In the Gallatin Valley and some other areas, it may be too late for good planning. Since so many resources and acres have already been devoted to inappropriate uses, trying to regulate development now would be difficult, to say the least. However, local residents should still push for complete and stringent planning to preserve an area's remaining natural values and local life style.

Hopefully, the grizzly will get high priority in forthcoming plans. If so, incompatible, economically doubtful, energy-extravagant, incompletely planned developments like Ski Yellowstone can be averted in the review process.

WHEN LESS IS MORE

The steady encroachment into Old Ephraim's strongholds directly reflects America's wasteful life styles. As a throwaway society continues to demand more resources and space, grizzly country continues to shrink — since these resources and space end up coming from the last wild lands.

As a general rule, "small is beautiful" should replace the "bigger is better" philosophy that contaminates the majority of Americans. Resource and energy conservation benefits the nation, its people, and its grizzlies. But Americans are addicted to trash compacters, electric hair dryers, shaving cream heaters, more cars than a family needs, a dozen yardlights burning all night over freeway rest stops, electric doors, glass office buildings whose windows can't be opened, electric outdoor advertising, two dozen color TVs blaring away all day at K-Mart, snow blowers, gas guzzling racing cars and cabin cruisers, street lights that come on a half-hour before darkness or on cloudy days, electric knives, riding lawn mowers, flying Winnebagos, more than one home per family, escalators going all day in stairless shopping malls, and more. The list seems endless. And not nearly enough people associate this waste with the grizzly's plight. Would westerners give up

167

Do outdoor-minded people need such extravagance to enjoy the great outdoors? Would they give it up to help the grizzly? Beth Givens photo.

gas-hungry, four-wheel-drive pickups to save energy and help the grizzly?

Aldo Leopold said it best: "To build a road is so much simpler than to think of what the country really needs."

GRAZING ALLOTMENTS

The Forest Service and, to a lesser degree, the Bureau of Land Management allow livestock to graze grizzly habitat around Yellowstone Park. The extent of predation has undoubtedly been exaggerated. But the bear has certainly caused stockmen some economic suffering.

Today, preserving the grizzly has higher priority than a dozen or so grazing allotments around Yellowstone Park. Public land grazing can continue elsewhere, but in these few areas, it should be phased out. Nearly every authority studying the grizzly situation, including the National Academy of Sciences, has recommended against sheep grazing around Yellowstone. Nonetheless, it continues.

If the stock isn't pulled out, ranchers will have to accept any loss from grizzlies as part of the grazing arrangement. The present situation, in which Old Ephraim gets blown away every time he eyes sheep grazing his domain, is intolerable. After all, grazing public land is a *privilege,* not a *right.* Regrettably, even this compromise — grazing with no predator control — probably won't work, since sheepmen will continue to slaughter bears.

THE MEDIA

"The grizzly bear, like airplane crashes and natural disasters, make good copy," Dr. Charles Jonkel observes. "In fact, the grizzly embodies two things journalistically attractive: its fearsome, violent reputation and its role as a symbol of the natural world."

The big bear is big news. Without zealous media coverage, efforts to save the grizzly wouldn't be as successful as they have been. However, the media must report grizzly news accurately, as must the publications and other communication outlets of environmental organizations.

The *news* media must, of course, try to report objectively. Reporters shouldn't downplay an exciting story even if it isn't exactly the *best* story as far as the grizzly is concerned.

"People get killed out there on that road almost every week, and I can't even find anything about it in the paper," an administrator at Glacier Park recently complained. "But if a hiker even gets *scratched* by a grizzly, it's all

169

over the nation."

It's an unavoidable characteristic of the news media to emphasize the part of the story most eagerly read by subscribers — in this case, the grizzly's fierce nature. Although this overstatement hinders the bear's struggle to survive, changes in news coverage of grizzly maulings can't be expected. However, some reporters, to be sure, could use greater discretion in re-counting stories of grizzlies.

Reporters have an obligation to report news, and grizzly maulings are big news, bigger than news of thousands of ghastly automobile accidents filling the back page of newspapers. Grizzly maulings are bigger news than car wrecks both because they're rare and because they feed the American desire to know the bloody details when grizzly and man meet. Rare and newsworthy, bear maulings will continue to attract attention in front page slots, while gruesome car disasters are passed over with scarcely a glance.

On the other hand, many environmental publications and writers, eager to urge the grizzly's preservation, have actually hurt the bear's cause. In their editorials and articles, they have made inaccurate assessments or overem-phasized less important aspects of the grizzly's dilemma. In fact, they have often had an effect opposite to their avowed purpose, to save the silvertip.

The overemphasis on hunting offers the best example of a misguided approach to preservation efforts, and Lewis Regenstein, of the Fund for Animals, provides a perfect case in point by writing, "In fact, the virtually unrestricted trophy hunting of grizzlies in the national forests of Montana, and to a lesser extent of Wyoming, is the single greatest threat to the survival of these animals."

This is, of course, nonsense — hunting is hardly "the single greatest threat" to the grizzly or to any other game animal. Nonetheless, if a national poll were taken right now asking what the greatest threat to the grizzly is, "hunting" would probably emerge as the most frequent answer.

It's clearly time for preservationists to relax their attack on hunting and to urge federal agencies to protect habitat and to help educate the public about the grizzly's true character. Dozens of national and local environmental groups are working to save the silvertip. These organizations are filled with wonderful public-spirited people who freely take time from their busy lives to protect the natural world. However, concentrating effort on banning hunting gets nowhere — except perhaps into a squabble with a wildlife club or game department. Sportsmen, game departments, *and* environmental groups should fight for the grizzly instead of with each other.

The hunting question has deep roots and deserves an answer. But not

170

now. Present regulations aren't "wiping out the species," as some critics claim. It's important to put aside this debate and concentrate instead on slowing down widespread exploitation of grizzly country. And by all means, environmental publications should reflect this new philosophy.

It would be a sad story for America's most magnificent mammal if conservationists spent the next 25 years fighting over hunting or other less significant issues while habitat encroachment continued unabated.

PUBLIC EDUCATION

Most efforts to help the grizzly falter because they lack a carefully conceived, extensive public information campaign. Although most officials responsible for grizzly management recognize the importance of keeping the public informed, bureaucracies just don't have the time or public relations experience to get the full story to the public. Although officials will undoubtedly become more open in responding to reasonable requests, there is need for full-fledged information programs.

Back in July 1974, Charles Jonkel supported this view in an official letter to the Montana Department of Fish and Game. "Popular articles representing the state's position and stressing the importance of game management in the preservation of the species are required as soon as possible." John Craighead emphasized the same point: "You won't decide any issue, unless you can get it before the public." (For example, a major transplant project won't succeed without a total information effort.)

Unfortunately, public information efforts have, at times, been self-serving. For example, the Park Service has given out a story that made park bear programs and policy look praiseworthy, holding back the real story or the one that benefited the grizzly most. Without open, honest information from official sources, the public automatically suspects bureaucratic bungling.

A CENTRAL ISSUE

To work up any enthusiasm to fight for the grizzly one must first want the silvertip's salvation. To a hard core bear-lover, this concept sounds incredible. Nonetheless, many people in grizzly country want bear numbers low and bears confined to national parks. Others wouldn't shed a single tear if the last silvertip disappeared.

Obviously, public tolerance emerges as a central issue. If the public doesn't want grizzlies, the species doesn't have a chance. Therefore, public education on the bear's behavior and significance is paramount in preserv-

171

ing the species.

On May 30, 1974, a female grizzly and her three cubs came down out of western Montana's Mission Mountains and killed five sheep near Pablo. The sheepmen shot the stock killer, and the three cubs scrambled up a 100-foot spruce.

A few hours later, local game wardens Ron Carlson, Dale Graff, and Larry Deist arrived and tried to capture the new orphans. The tree was too tall, however, so they left a live trap at the foot of the tree. The next morning they found two of the cubs in the trap, but the third one had escaped.

About this time the landowner, Willard Crockett, came by. "And he wanted to kill those cubs," exclaimed game warden Dale Graff. After a heated exchange, the wardens took the cubs and left.

Later, Crockett was asked *why* he felt so strongly, since the cubs wouldn't destroy his livestock. "They sure and hell would when they got bigger," he snapped. "They're not afraid of man anymore. They're the worst kind. Same way with coyotes and the whole bunch — the only good one is a dead one when they're in trouble."

Crockett was also asked if he would prefer not to have any grizzlies in the entire area. "You bet your life I would," Crockett returned. "And if they get on my land and get in trouble, I'm not asking [the game department] whether I can shoot them or not. I'm going to kill them."

"If you fellows had to do the paying, you wouldn't want so many grizzly bears," he concluded.

Crockett's views are widespread among western landowners. And they have a strong argument that has been reinforced through history, growing stronger every time a predator kills domestic stock. This age-old conflict between man and predator has fostered much of today's bitterness against wildlife, especially predators, and against wildlife agencies and citizen groups working to preserve endangered species. Unfortunately, grizzly bears are classed with drug rehabilitation centers and homes for unwed mothers — most people approve of them as long as they're somewhere else.

Although there are many options for a concerned citizenry to save grizzlies and their habitat, there remains the important question of what happens to a grizzly that comes down into an inhabited area and causes property damage on private land. Certainly, the private landowner shouldn't be expected to absorb the damages, especially if a bear is an habitual troublemaker.

In attempting to find a solution to this sticky situation, some conservationists have suggested compensating the property owner for damage caused by grizzlies. But this is out of the question for the following reasons: 1) Such programs have in the past been riddled by corruption — even

172

though a cow or sheep has died of natural causes, from disease, or from eating poisonous plants, stockmen have been able to collect damages by claiming that a predator killed the animal. 2) Landowners would have to prove without doubt that a grizzly had done the damage, which is no trivial task. 3) Some bears are habitual stock killers — the government can't continue to compensate indefinitely for the damage these animals do.

As civilization makes further inroads into grizzly country and the bear's habitat shrinks, more and more bears will become problems as they're forced into civilization's camps by population stress in the grizzly hierarchy. So what should authorities do with problem bears? Should a bad bear be killed? If so, how? Sometimes, the public won't accept the idea of a government control agent shooting, trapping, or poisoning such a bear. Hardly more palatable to the public is the idea of removing problem bears by hunting, although carefully controlled hunting could help alleviate the problem by removing surplus bears.

Steve Bayless, of the Montana Department of Fish and Game, has another idea. "When it comes to livestock predations, I think we should let hunters do it. I mean as soon as we find out there's a bear causing problems, call the hunter who has the next permit and tell him to get over there quick. We could have these sportsmen lined up in advance." But Bayless's idea will arouse negative reactions because of its "hired gun" image.

The only answer is destroy these problem bears. But how? A well-monitored harvest seems more pleasing than the image of the majestic grizzly eating strychnine, agonizing in a leghold trap, or watching a rifle barrel slowly edge through the iron mesh of a live trap and then exploding. However, such a harvest will probably get shot down upon public scrutiny.

So in the end, authorities are left with a big bear problem with no politically acceptable solution.

Chapter 7

DO WE REALLY NEED
GRIZZLY BEARS?

The drama of the great white bear could be in its last act. The "horrible bear" of the western wilderness is still fighting for his life, for the right to roam wild and free, as in ages past.

There are a few cautious optimists in the audience. "We have Yellowstone, Glacier, and Grand Teton national parks and the Bob Marshall, Scapegoat, and Washakie wilderness areas," they point out. "Even if we lose the bear in the Cabinet, Mission, Spanish Peaks, Beartooth, Madison, and Whitefish mountain ranges, and in Idaho and Washington, we'll still have a few grizzlies. Perhaps that's all society will tolerate."

However, the optimists' theory doesn't consider the biological axiom that a species existing as remnant populations in small, isolated habitats is particularly vulnerable. When so reduced, the species may not survive a natural or artificial disaster. In fact, in such population the death of a single individual can plunge the species into extinction. This "point of no return" can be reached without anyone's realizing it. Then, in a few years after the survivors gradually die out, the earth has lost another creature.

On the other hand, a widespread, healthy population, which can travel freely, can more easily withstand environmental stress. It can more easily adapt to changing conditions.

Optimists also say that even if Old Ephraim disappears from the lower 48 states, Canada and Alaska will still have lots of grizzly bears. Perhaps Aldo Leopold answered this theory best by writing, "There seems to be a tacit assumption that if grizzlies survive in Canada and Alaska, that is good enough. It is not good enough for me. Relegating grizzlies to Alaska is about like relegating happiness to Heaven; one may never get there."

Many people who have lived in grizzly country take a dark view of the bear's future. They have listened to too much anti-grizzly sentiment at public meetings; argued with too many developers; experienced with dismay too many destructive technological trends; watched with dismay extravagant life styles become even more wasteful; heard too many Chambers of Commerce champion every development; and seen too many grandiose schemes win public and political approval. They know from experience that the big bear is threatened on all fronts. They know also that without drastic preventive action, America will lose the grizzly south of Canada and that with the bear will go a source of national pride.

But how do we convince the poor, unemployed, or hungry that the grizzly can be saved by preserving millions of acres of wilderness? Because the big bear's plight is certainly overshadowed by the endless anguish of malnutrition and poverty, should Old Ephraim be allowed to pass away and his domain be used to help the impoverished?

Undoubtedly, the American people are capable of extracting and consuming their last natural resource regardless of environmental expense. They are able to continue promoting high-density recreational development in the remaining quiet places. Our technocrats can easily do this — they only need a green light. And conservationists, including myself, who have repeatedly pushed for preserving the grizzly would be more inclined to tolerate this loss *if* they thought for one moment those resources and recreational opportunities would alleviate unemployment, humanize ghettos, feed the starving, and make economic opportunity equitable.

However, under the present system, the last wild places would go under for neon, snowmobiles, trash mashers, second-home condominiums, electric toothbrushes, gondolas, electrically heated swimming pools, no deposit/no return beverage containers, platinum jewelry, and needless luxuries. Can we in good conscience send Old Ephraim to his grave so too many Americans can ride elevators up two floors, watch garage doors open electronically, or have a bigger bathtub?

Bad developments like Ski Yellowstone, which permanently shrink the grizzly's domain, can be condoned, but they won't help cure cultural ills. These are *second home* subdivisions, which only the affluent can purchase, while many Americans can barely afford *one* home. And what of the thousands who can't scrape together the down payment for *any kind of home?* Since only the well-to-do can afford to fly or drive to distant recreational resorts like Ski Yellowstone, how can these developments possibly be justified in a time of energy and natural resource scarcity, of economic inequity, and of urgency for the great bear?

It's possible to build roads and power lines through vital grizzly habitat to Big Sky and at the same time encourage the rapid, haphazard development of the entire Gallatin Canyon. But this "progress" does nothing for thousands of disadvantaged Americans. Both the power line and road discussed in Chapter 5 only make it easier for the wealthy to get to — and live more comfortably in — Big Sky, which is already a giant playground for the affluent.

Coal fields can be developed in the Flathead Valley, rendering a large area useless for grizzlies. But the resulting energy won't go to the ghettos for mass transit or heating. It won't even go to heat schools, hospitals, and homes for the middle-class. It will go to Japanese steel mills

Every sawlog on every public forest could be cut. But would the wood products go to build decent housing for the poor? Or would they go into second home condominiums?

Developers often say they want to help the poor, provide jobs, and benefit the local community. And when I hear such talk, I think of an earlier trip to Big Sky. While researching a magazine article, I asked if tent camping were allowed in the resort's $6-a-night, mobile home "campground." The tour guide responded; "No. We don't want that kind of people here."

If one trims away the verbiage, there remains the somber fact that Americans aren't wiping out the wilderness king's domain to relieve a national need or cure any social sickness. The wilderness is being destroyed only to maintain an already-too-high life style for the already-too-affluent. And even all-out exploitation can merely maintain this unrestrained living for a short period. In a few years, the depletion of resources will finally force a change, but too late for Old Ephriam. Why can't we change now, while there's a chance to preserve some of the greatest nation's natural integrity and its most magnificent wild creature?

The American system is based on continued economic growth and industrial productivity. The more growth there is, the more goods people consume, and the more they waste and throw away — all the better for the country's economic health. Religiously tied to this concept, Americans steadily whittle away the wilderness, driving the mighty grizzly to extinction.

With blinders on, Americans push to exploit the earth, with no regard for the future. A few want to change, but change is difficult at best, as the entire nation is caught in a disastrous form of perpetual motion. Without a "small is beautiful," "less is more" ethic, which calls for resource recovery and conservation, Americans are headed for destruction along with Old Ephraim.

Even America's greatest wildernesses — British Columbia, the Yukon Territory, and Alaska — are in jeopardy. Once while discussing this threat with an Alaskan friend, he pooh-poohed the idea, "It's so big; they could never do it." How incredibly naive that sounds after observing what happened to the western United States in a scant 150 years and sensing what the plans for the next 50 are.

Mike Frome, former conservation editor of *Field & Stream* and *American Forests* and author of several books, puts the trend in sharp perspective: "Instead of husbanding and carefully cultivating our raw materials, so that we can live off the interest while saving the capital stock, this generation is digging voraciously into the capital as though there is no tomorrow. The so-called advanced or developed — or perhaps I should say *overdeveloped* — nations are the worst offenders, and none more guilty than the United States.

"We are, in this age, robbing the rest of the world in order to sustain our own unbalanced affluent and wasteful society." As Frome so aptly notes, Americans simply must consume less. And they can do it without undue personal sacrifice.

Author/scientist Renne Dubos says, "in any kind of society, the healthiest, happiest, and most creative persons are likely to be found among those who consume least." There must be a return to basic living, where life will be happier and healthier, instead of a race to sustain a throwaway age.

Perhaps the greatest tragedy of all is the failure to accept the grizzly's disappearance as a step toward mankind's eventual demise, the failure to realize that man is inescapably linked in delicate equilibrium, to other forms of life. As John Muir once said: when one tugs on a single thing in nature, he finds it attached to the rest of the world.

As man destroys the habitat of any creature, he is destroying his own habitat. Each attack on the environment kicks a negative repercussion into motion, and some day, we might not be able to stop this chain reaction. The day the grizzly vanishes won't mark the day the sky falls, but it will be a certain sign of man's failure to comprehend the future.

Actually, we're fortunate to have wild animals like the grizzly to act as a barometer of environmental quality. By keeping the world livable for wildlife, man assures it will be livable for himself, his children, and their children. A strip mine can, at best, serve people for a few decades. But as grizzly habitat, the land can serve them forever.

Before technology made it unnecessary, miners took canaries into the depths with them. When a canary died, they scrambled to the surface for pure air. They knew that the air in the mine was bad, and they would die next. Likewise, we should closely watch our "canaries." We have so many of them, all the wild creatures around us. However, when they start dying, we may not have a protective surface to scramble to.

Old Ephraim's demise could mean another step toward the loss of smokeless skies, scenic vistas, free rivers, grass oceans, silence, easy smiles, elbow room. It could mean that the Rocky Mountain West had become America's second home and that total resource utilization prevailed.

If Americans can't conserve resources and energy or curb civilization's lemming-like advance into grizzly country, if grizzly advocates can't be convinced that the preservation of habitat is the central issue of the bear's salvation, if the public cannot learn to tolerate the bear, if the federal government (especially the Forest Service) won't put the bear first in land use decisions, and if scientists are unable to work together for the grizzly's benefit, then surely the wild grizzly will disappear.

Although there will still be grizzlies in zoos, the species will, in essence, be extinct. When the wild, free-roaming grizzly disappears, the fight is over. The pitiful bears condemned to zoos might have a remote chance of surviving the wilds, but if their release were proposed, local residents would probably block any concerted effort to restore them to suitable habitat. Confined grizzlies would have become so accustomed to man, it would be difficult to convince protesters that property damage wouldn't result.

Fathers, like myself, used to constantly fret about leaving a sizeable estate — a big house, a tract of fertile land, a fat bank account, and other material and financial commodities — to their offspring. I prefer to leave *very few* material possessions *and* a healthy environment, of which the grizzly bear would be an essential part. The preservation of the grizzly and his domain is a long-term investment, an act of faith that unborn generations will never cease to appreciate.

Yes, we really need grizzly bears.

Afterword

THE REQUIEM SOUND

Everyone has experiences that last a lifetime — precious moments, often recalled and becoming more meaningful as the years hurry by. I have had two such experiences, with the king of the American wilderness, which clearly define the grizzly's place in modern America.

In 1967, I was working in the backcountry of Glacier Park. That particular morning seemed routine, but it hardly turned out that way.

After hiking several miles, my companion and I came to a wild mountain stream. My partner stopped for a cold drink and joked as I almost fell crossing to the opposite bank on a fallen lodgepole pine conveniently extending from bank to bank. Once across, I filled my hard hat with ice-cold water, downed it, and leaned back to drift into one of those momentary daydreams that come so easily in pristine places.

After a few seconds, I was rudely brought back to reality by my partner's frantic pointing upstream. The roar of the rushing water stole his words, but he was obviously startled. Peeking over the branches of the lodgepole, I saw why, and the movie camera of my mind registering a few seconds for all future daydreams.

There, knee-deep in wild water was a large female grizzly helping a cub across the treacherous rapids. Her other cub was already across. Carefully, the female monarch half-carried, half-pushed her offspring through the icy torrent. Only 50 yards away, the royal family seemed uncomfortably close.

Then, in a movement almost too fast to follow, the mother was on guard. Her nose went up — trying to identify the foreign scent some tattletale breeze had brought her.

She seemed exactly in the right place, her huge hulk silhouetted against the blue sky and the snowy crags of the northern Livingstone Range. Here was the wilderness hallmark — a silvertip amid unspoiled scenery, ready to defend her cubs, which innocently played nearby. Although the roaring waterway made so much noise we couldn't hear each other at 20 feet, the scene was strangely silent.

Again, the breeze brought her the suspicious scent, and the bears bolted across the stream, quickly melting into the forest. Since speed blurred the details, I have always wondered how the cubs forded the stream so rapidly when a few seconds earlier they had needed help.

We fled. Later, after momentary fear had subsided, I realized how fortunate I had been. Very few people will ever see a wild grizzly. Although many people will peer at a prideless grizzly in a zoo, only a handful will ever view Old Ephraim in a wilderness setting.

That day, I saw America's strength, courage, and lifeblood embodied in a magnificent animal. I saw a remnant of the wilderness on which the country has been built. I saw the wild world working the way it is supposed to — in matchless harmony. If I am ever asked to describe a scene of total beauty, serenity, and peace, I will surely recount those few seconds.

True, not many people will ever view a grizzly in a comparable setting, but this is of little importance. Even if *no one* were to witness such a scene, it will endure in our consciousness. Just knowing that somewhere a mother grizzly is helping her cubs across a mountain stream in a primeval wilderness can help us maintain stability and security.

In later years, I saw several grizzlies on backcountry trails. Without exception, they fled like spooked cottontails upon sensing my presence. Before long, I caught myself wishing a bear wouldn't immediately run away — so I could get a better look. My inherent fear soon changed to awe and admiration, and even to jealousy. Unequivocally, the grizzly symbolizes the spirit of the wilderness.

But this spirit is slipping away from us. The grizzly stands for an endangered heritage that the nation can ill afford to sacrifice to a high "standard of living." We must somehow preserve the harmony I experienced along that mountain stream.

Just as I saw nature at its best that spring day, I have seen nature at its worst — the outcome of our greed to conquer the wilderness. I have heard the requiem sound.

In the spring of 1973, a different female grizzly and her two cubs wandered into a campground in Glacier Park. They were tranquilized and moved into the park's interior — far away from campgrounds and "safe," everybody thought.

Twelve days later, a stockman shot the female near Bigfork, Montana, about 75 air miles away, after she had allegedly killed one sheep. What compelled the wilderness queen to take her cubs and flee the park's security, swim the Middle Fork of the Flathead River, climb the Great Northern Mountains, swim either the Hungry Horse Reservoir or the South Fork of the Flathead River, cross the Swan Range, and enter the more populated Flathead Valley remains a mystery. But it meant the end of this royal family.

After the assassination, game wardens found the two cubs huddled helplessly nearby. Too young to survive without a mother, the orphans were brought to the game department's Helena office. Their new "home" was an eight-foot-square, concrete-floored cubicle in the department's shelter for orphaned wildlife. Their cage was only a stone's throw from my office. So I could hear them bawling, as people filed past their pen, exclaiming how "cute" the cubs were, but missing the significance of what they saw.

Others from my office regularly visited the shelter, but I could muster the courage only two or three times. As I looked through the steel mesh and the cubs stared back, I could only think of the grizzlies I had seen in earlier years — and especially those two cubs crossing the wild stream. Those cubs had been exactly in the right place, and these were exactly in the wrong place. Just as I will always remember those few seconds when I had been mesmerized by the majestic mother and her family, I won't forget these staredowns with the two orphans.

At first, they cowered in the corner, sulking, and looking thoroughly pitiful. On occásion, they charged the confining steel, clawing and crying out. Ever so slowly, though, they adapted to their artificial environment. Their fierce tenacity for life apparently overcame their fear of man. They gradually accepted food and drink. And they began adjusting to their new surroundings.

181

This was hard on me. These two young animals which seemed so synonymous with wildness would apparently give up their wild birthright to survive — even if it meant a lifetime of exile. For the two young grizzlies, there would be no going back to their proper place — the splendor of Glacier's wilderness. I even considered bringing my rifle and finishing them right there. It would have been better for them.

I didn't, however, and the zookeeper came and carried the cubs away to a prideless maturity in a big city zoo. Certainly, this must be a fate worse than death for the wild grizzly.

After enjoying a few brief months of wildness, the prince and princess were condemned to a cage where they must endure hordes of humans trooping by, gawking across the moat, tossing in peanuts, but not understanding. Hopefully, the memory of their momentary freedom is etched too dimly on their minds to haunt them.

If the mighty grizzly, the symbol of the wilderness, our most magnificent mammal, ever perishes, this is how the final curtain will fall. The requiem sound will be the merciful whimper of a homeless, caged cub.

Department of Fish and Game photo.

183

BIBLIOGRAPHY

Books

Bailey, Vernon. *Mammals of North Dakota.* U.S. Department of Agriculture. Biological Survey. 1926.

Bailey, Vernon. *Mammals of New Mexico.* U.S. Department of Agriculture. Biological Survey. December, 1931.

Bailey, Vernon. *Biological Survey of Texas.* U.S. Department of Agriculture. Biological Survey. Government Printing Office. 1905.

Bell, Major Horace. *On the Old West Coast.* Edited by Lanier Bartlett. New York. William Morrow and Company, Inc. 1930.

Cockrum, E.L. *Mammals of Kansas.* University of Kansas Publications, Museum of Natural History. Vol. 7. August 25, 1952.

Cowan, Ian McTaggart and Guiguet, Charles J. *The Mammals of British Columbia.* Department of Recreation and Conservation. Handbook No. 11. October, 1965.

DeVoto, Bernard. (Ed.) *The Journals of Lewis and Clark.* Boston. Houghton Mifflin Company. 1953.

Frome, Michael. *Battle for the Wilderness.* New York and Washington. Praeger Publishers. 1974.

Haynes, Bessie and Edgar. *The Grizzly Bear.* Norman. University of Oklahoma Press. 1966.

Leopold, Aldo. *A Sand County Almanac.* Oxford University Press. 1949.

Leopold, A. Starker. *Wildlife in Mexico: The Game Birds and Mammals.* University of California Press, Berkeley and Los Angeles and Cambridge University Press, London. 1959.

McCracken, Harold. *The Beast That Walks Like A Man.* Garden City, New York. Hanover House. 1955.

Mills, Enos A. *The Grizzly: Our Greatest Wild Animal.* Boston and New York. Houghton Mifflin Company. 1919.

185

Muir, Jean. *The Adventures of Grizzly Adams.* New York. Putman. 1969.

Olsen, Jack. *The Night of the Grizzlies.* New York. Putman. 1969.

Robinson, Doane. *Encyclopedia of South Dakota.* Pierre. Published by Author. 1925.

Russell, Andy. *Grizzly Country.* New York, Alfred A. Knopf. 1968.

Schoonmaker, Walter. *The World of the Grizzly Bear.* Lippincott. 1968.

Stevens, Montague. *Meet Mr. Grizzly.* Albuquerque. The University of New Mexico Press. 1944.

Storer, Tracey I. and Trevis, Lloyd P. Jr. *California Grizzly.* Berkeley and Los Angeles. University of California Press. 1955.

Wright, William Henry. *The Grizzly Bear.* New York. Charles Scribner's Sons. 1909.

Magazine and Newspaper Articles

Albert, Gene. "Glacier: Beleaguered Park of 1975." *National Parks & Conservation.* November, 1975.

Arbour, Vince. "Bears and The Man." *Earth.* November, 1971.

"Bad Management Hurts Grizzly." *Jackson Hole News.* October 17, 1975.

Brewster, William. "When bears awaken, biologists go on the prowl." *High Country News.* May 7, 1976.

Burk, Dale. "The Grizzly is Threatened." *The Missoulian.* March 20, 1975.

Byard, Jane. "A Time of Horror..." *The Missoulian.* September 24, 1976.

Cauble, Christopher. "How Do You Travel in Grizzly Country? Very Carefully!" *Sports Afield.* July, 1976.

Clark, Frank. "The Killing of Old Ephraim." *Utah Fish and Game Bulletin.* Utah Fish and Game Department. September, 1952.

Chadwick, Douglas. "Dreams of the Great Bear." *Defenders.* February, 1976.

Cole, Glen F. "Management Involving Grizzly Bears and Humans in Yellowstone National Park." 1970-73. *BioScience.* June, 1974.

Craighead, Frank Jr. "They're Killing Yellowstone's Grizzlies." Interviewed in *National Wildlife.* October[November, 1973

Dobson, Ed. "Grizzly Habitat Still Shrinking: Action Needed." *Not Man Apart.* Friends of the Earth. Mid-September, 1975.

Finley, William L. and Irene. "To Feed or Not to Feed — That is the Bear Question." *American Forests.* August, 1940.

Frome, Michael. "Do Grizzlies Face a Grisly Future?" *Field & Stream.* January, 1974.

Frome, Michael. "The Grizzly's Needs Should Come Before Man's." *Defenders.* February, 1976.

Frome, Michael. "Crusade for Wildlife." *Defenders of Wildlife News.* April, 1975.

Garrett, Tom. "Why Grizzlies Should be on the Threatened List." *Not Man Apart.* Friends of the Earth. April, 1975.

Gilbert, Bil. "The Great Grizzly Controversy." *Audubon.* January, 1976.

Gould, Laurence M. "Park Service Thwarts Work on Grizzly Bears." *The Missoulian. November 5, 1975.*

"The Grizzly Debate." National Parks & Conservation. April, 1975.

Herrero, Stephen. "Human Injury Inflicted by Grizzly Bears." *Science.* November 6, 1970.

Herrero, Stephen. "Man and the Grizzly Bear (present, past, but future?)." *BioScience.* Vol. 20, No. 21. November 1, 1970.

Housholder, Bob. "The Grizzly Bear in Arizona." *Arizona Wildlife Sportsman.* July, 1961.

Humbird, Jim. "Grizzly Hunt Ban Next Step?" *Fishing and Hunting News.* July 20, 1974.

Johnson, A. Stephen. "Yellowstone's Grizzlies: Endangered or Prospering?" *Defenders of Wildlife News.* October, 1973.

Johnson, A. Stephen. "Man, Grizzly & National Parks." *National Parks & Conservation.* February, 1972.

Jonkel, Charles. "Of Men and Bears." *Western Wildlands.* School of Forestry, University of Montana. Winter, 1975.

Jonkel, Charles. "Media Coverage Threatens Grizzlies." *Montana Kaimin.* University of Montana. October 17, 1975.

Lachenmeier, Rudy R. "The Endangered Species Act of 1973: Preservation or Pandemonium?" *Environmental Law.* The Lewis and Clark Law School. Northwestern School of Law. Portland. Fall, 1974.

Malloy, Michael T. "Bear Fight Bares Few Bear Facts." *National Observer.* November 24, 1973.

"Managing the Grizzly: Department Position Statement." *Montana Outdoors.* Montana Department of Fish and Game. September[October, 1975.

Mitchell, John G. "Bear at the Brink." *Sports Afield.* February, 1976.

Moment, Gairdner B. "Bears and Conservation: Realities and Recommendations." *BioScience.* November, 1969.

Moment, Gairdner B. "Bears: The Need for a New Sanity in Wildlife Conservation." *BioScience.* December, 1968.

Rearden, Jim. "The Status of Alaska's Big Bears." *Outdoor Life.* May, 1976.

Regenstein, Lewis. "Heading for the Last Hibernation." *New York Times.* January 24, 1975.

"Report on Yellowstone grizzly study rejects 'facing extinction' charge." *National Park Service Newsletter.* September, 1974.

Roop, Larry. "What are we doing about the Yellowstone grizzly?" *Wyoming Wildlife.* Wyoming Game and Fish Department. April, 1975.

Russell, Andy. "Grizzly Country...a vanishing heritage." *BC Outdoors.* February, 1976.

Russell, Andy. "Are Grizzlies Man Killers?" *BC Outdoors.* December, 1968.

Schneider, Bill. "The Grizzly." *Montana Outdoors.* Montana Department of Fish and Game. July[August, 1975.

Schneider, Bill. "The Mighty Grizzly...What Does the Future Hold?" *Western Outdoors.* October, 1975.

Schneider, Bill. "The Story Behind the Grizzly Bear Controversy." *Empire Magazine. The Denver Post.* November 16, 1975.

Schneider, Bill. "Will This Grizzly Attack?" *National Wildlife.* February[March, 1977.

Schneider, Bill. "The Grizzly: Is He Villain or Victim?" *Outdoor Life.* November, 1976.

Schneider, Bill. "The Ski Yellowstone Proposal." *Montana Outdoors.* Montana Department of Fish and Game. November[December, 1974.

Schneider, Bill. "The Gallatin: A Good Chance to Question Growth or Another Splendor to Squander?" *Montana Outdoors.* Montana Department of Fish and Game. January[February, 1975.

Seater, Stephen R. "Vanishing Point: The Grizzly Bear." *Environmental Quality magazine.* July, 1973.

Seater, Stephen R. "Grizzly at Bay." *National Parks & Conservation.* November, 1975.

Sheely, Terry. "Fund, Feds Did Job on Montana Grizzlies." *Fishing and Hunting News.* May 18, 1974.

Stingley, Jim. "Survival Issue: Grizzly: Men Fight to Death — Maybe His." *Los Angeles Times.* February 5, 1973.

Taylor, Ted. M. "Vanished Monarch of the Sierra." *The American West.* May[June, 1976.

Walcheck, Ken. "Lewis and Clark Meet the Awesome White Bear." *Montana Outdoors.* Montana Department of Fish and Game. September[October, 1976.

Zaccagnini, Ronald. "Is the Grizzly Gone?" *Colorado Outdoors.* Colorado Division of Wildlife. July[August, 1975.

Zochert, Donald. "Grizzly Attacks Remain a Mystery." *Chicago Daily News.* October 10, 1976.

Technical Reports and Government Documents

Allen, Arthur and Jorgensen, Carole. "Grizzly Bear Study: Targhee National Forest." Unpublished report available from the Targhee National Forest. U.S. Forest Service. October 31, 1975.

Cole, Glen F. "Management Involving Grizzly Bears in Yellowstone National Park 1970-72." National Park Service, U.S. Department of the Interior. Natural Resources Report Number 7. 1973.

Chadwick, Douglas H. "Grizzly Bear Survey in a Selected Portion of the Swan Range of Western Montana." Graduate research study. University of Montana, Missoula. 1974.

Craighead, John J., Varney, Joel R. and Craighead, Frank C. Jr. "A Population Analysis of the Yellowstone Grizzly Bears." University of Montana, Missoula. September, 1974.

The Endangered Species Act of 1973.

Erickson, Albert W. "Evaluation of the Suitability of the Gila Wilderness for Re-establishment of the Grizzly Bear." Supported by the U.S. Forest Service. September, 1974.

Erickson, Albert W. "Grizzly Bear Management in the Seeley Lake Ranger District." Supported by the U.S. Forest Service. Lolo National Forest. June, 1975.

"The Facts About Ski Yellowstone Mountain Lake Resort." Ski Yellowstone, Inc. 1974.

"Framework for the Future — Forest Service Objectives and Policy Guides." U.S. Department of Agriculture. 1970.

Greer, Ken. "Job Progress Report — May 1, 1974 through December 31, 1974." Montana Department of Fish and Game. September 30, 1975.

Griffel, David. "Bear — Livestock Interactions of the Targhee National Forest." Unpublished report available from the Targhee National Forest. 1976.

"Grizzly Bear Management Plan." Montana Department of Fish and Game. October 12, 1973.

"Grizzly Bear Attacks At Granite Park and Trout Lake in Glacier National Park. August 13, 1967." National Park Service, U.S. Department of the Interior.

"Hebgen Lake Estates: A Proposed Subdivision in Gallatin County." Draft Environmental Impact Statement. Montana Department of Health and Environmental Sciences. September 23, 1974.

"Hebgen Lake Planning Unit." Draft Environmental Impact Statement. U.S. Forest Service. Gallatin National Forest. December 4, 1974.
"Hebgen Lake Planning Unit." Final Environmental Impact Statement. U.S. Forest Service. Gallatin National Forest. November 13, 1975.

"Hebgen Lake Land Use Plan — 1974 with Management Options." U.S. Forest Service. Gallatin National Forest. Spring, 1974.

Haglund, Brent M. "Impact of Ski Yellowstone Development on Grizzly Bears." Written on request of Hans Geier, Ski Yellowstone, Inc. Spring, 1975.

Herrero, Stephen. "Conflicts between Man and Grizzly Bears in the National Parks of North America." Bears — Their Biology and Management. A selection of papers from the Third International Conference on Bear Research and Management. International Union for Conservation of Nature and Natural Resources. Morges, Switzerland. June, 1974.

"Hinderland Who's Who: The Grizzly." Canadian Wildlife Service. 1973.

Jacobsen, Robert D. "Legal Aspects of Critical Habitat Determinations." Office of Endangered Species. U.S. Fish and Wildlife Service. Washington, D.C. February, 1977.

Jonkel, Charles. "Annual Report: Border Grizzly Project." School of Forestry. University of Montana, Missoula. March, 1976.

Knight, Richard and others. "Yellowstone Grizzly Bear Investigations. Annual Report of the Interagency Study Team. 1975." National Park Service. U.S. Department of the Interior. Miscellaneous Report Number 9. July, 1976.

"Interagency Grizzly Bear Study." Annual Report. March, 1974.

Light, Jerome T. "Wildlife Habitat Management Statement." U.S. Forest Service. Gallatin National Forest. July 19, 1974.

Master Plan — Yellowstone National Park. National Park Service. U.S. Department of the Interior. 1973.

"Montana Land Development." The Montana Subdivision Inventory Project. Environmental Information Center. February, 1975.

Montana Department of Fish and Game. Draft Environmental Impact Statement: Addendum Number One to Project No. FG-22: Annual Statewise Harvest of Big Game Animals. July 2, 1975.

National Academy of Sciences. Report of the Committee on the Yellowstone Grizzlies. July, 1974.

"Oil & Gas Lease Applications, Exploration and Development." Draft Environmental Impact Statement. U.S. Forest Service. Flathead National Forest. June 19, 1975.

189

"Petition Before the U.S. Department of the Interior Urging Endangered Species Status for the Grizzly Bear." Fund for Animals, Inc. February 14, 1974.

"Petition Before the U.S. Department of the Interior in Response to a Previous Petition by the Fund for Animals, Inc." Wyoming Game and Fish Department. June 17, 1974.

Preliminary Development Plan: Ski Yellowstone." Ski Yellowstone, Inc. Beardsley, Davis Associates, Inc. October, 1973.

"Proposed Oil and Gas Leases: Coal Creek State Forest." Draft Environmental Impact Statement. Montana Department of State Lands and Montana Department of Natural Resources and Conservation. November, 1975.

"Position Paper: Grizzly Bear." U.S. Fish and Wildlife Service. Office of Endangered Species. 1975.

Pearson, Arthur M. "The Northern Interior Grizzly Bear, *Ursus arctos L.*" Canadian Wildlife Service. Report Series Number 34. 1975.

Schallenberger, Allen. "Review of Oil and Gas Exploitation Impacts on Grizzly Bears." (Draft Copy.) Border Grizzly Bear Project. School of Forestry. University of Montana, Missoula. February, 1977.

Seymour, George. "Grizzly Bear." California Department of Fish and Game.

Sharpe, Craig. "Room to Live." Film produced by the Montana Department of Fish and Game. December, 1975.

Stuart, David G. "Impacts of Large Recreational Developments Upon Semi-Primitive Environments: The Gallatin Canyon Case Study." Supported by the National Science Foundation and Montana State University. 1975.

Wyoming Highway Department. Final Environmental Impact Statement on the Clarks Fork Canyon Road. February 16, 1973.

AUTHOR'S NOTE

I'm employed by the Montana Department of Fish and Game, the state agency responsible for wildlife management in Montana. However, the department had no influence on the contents or conclusions of the book. *Where the Grizzly Walks* does *not* reflect department views or policies. In fact, it has been made very clear to me that my employer does *not* agree with some sections of the book.

Nonetheless, some individuals, organizations, agencies, or companies may try to associate it with the department. These interest groups have been successful in controlling and silencing government employees before whereas they have been unsuccessful in tailoring the private media to their viewpoint. Thus, by trying to make this appear as a department project, they hope to restore the traditional bureaucratic way of doing and saying as little as possible. This unfortunate reality has helped keep the public in the dark on many conservation issues, including grizzly management. In addition, public agencies have "cooperative agreements" that tend to restrict and generalize the flow of public information.

This problem encouraged me to write this book. I'm convinced a concerned and informed populace can preserve the grizzly. Hopefully, those who resent the grizzly's presence won't succeed in associating the book, a purely private project, with government functions. If they do, the real issue — the reasons and methods for preserving the grizzly — could get lost in the uproar.

Bill Schneider